FLESH & BLOOD

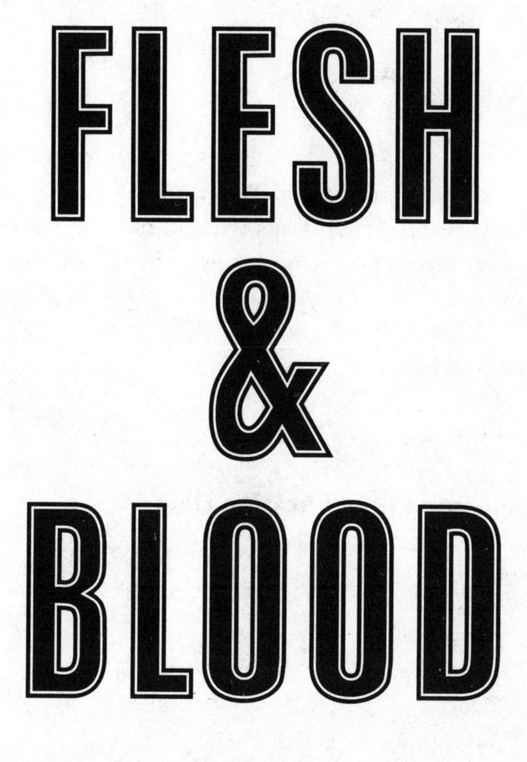

a journey into the heart of boxing

JIM CHRISTY

Douglas & McIntyre
Vancouver/Toronto

90 91 92 93 94 1 2 3 4 5

Douglas & McIntyre Ltd.
1615 Venables Street
Vancouver, British Columbia V5L 2H1

Canadian Cataloguing in Publication Data
Christy, Jim, 1945–
Flesh and blood
ISBN 0-88894-654-6
1. Boxing. I. Title.
GV1133.C48 1990 796.8'3 C90-091392-4

Edited by Barbara Pulling
Design by Alexandra Hass
Front jacket photograph by James LaBonté
Typesetting by The Typeworks

Printed and bound in Canada by D. W. Friesen & Sons Ltd.
Printed on acid-free paper ∞

For the old man

Two hours and more the fight had sped
  Near until ten it drew,
But still opposed one-armed to blind,
  They stood those dauntless two.
Ah, me! that I have lived to hear
  Such men as ruffians scorned,
Such deeds of valour "brutal" called,
  Canted, preached down and mourned!
Ah! that these old eyes ne'er again
  A gallant mill shall see!
No more behold the ropes and stakes
  With colours flying free.

William Makepeace Thackeray,
"The Fight of Sayerius and Heenanus,"
on the 1860 Sayers-Heenan heavyweight championship

Contents

FLESH & BLOOD

Reconnoitring an Uncommon Landscape

Noontime on a Wednesday in Vancouver's West End, and people in suits and smart dresses from government and engineering offices along Robson Street are headed to lunch in the market. If any of them notice us—and a few of them do—it is less because of Dave Cooke's red nylon ILWU windbreaker and 1955 rockabilly hairstyle than because of his walk, a walk that is no mere utilitarian placing of one foot in front of the other but rather a hyped-up, hustling gait, shoulders jerking as if he's being restrained by invisible hands from throwing short left hooks and neat right uppercuts. His motion through these streets calls to mind a deep-sea sailor just hit port, or a fighter anxious to make the centre of the ring and get the job done.

The other citizens no doubt peg him for a successful member of the working class, and they are partly right. Dave, aged forty-three, is a longshoreman who owns an apartment nearby and probably pulls down more dollars than the majority of the white-collar types around us. But his presence on the sunny street is more unusual than they might imagine. Even in this neighbourhood. Back there at the doors to the market, behind which a Russian guy awaits our return, are three gypsy women hustling the *gadja* while their men work the boutiques. The secondhand bookstore around the corner is run by a Lithuanian woman immigrant who spent ten years in the mountains of Tibet. The fellow at the counter of the convenience store tells harrowing tales of his flight from Idi Amin. You never know who you will find around here, especially with the immigration office only a block away—and that happens to be where we are headed. Nevertheless, Dave Cooke is in some ways a more exotic creature than all of these, for Dave is a fight guy, a boxing person.

The fight guy is fast being hustled off the North American stage. He is now sighted but rarely, like the red-crested kingfisher, the stand-up bass and the novelist who didn't come out of a creative writing school. But it wasn't all that long ago that fight guys were plentiful, roaming freely over the continent. In the fifties, when Dave Cooke was growing up in this very town, he could watch boxing matches on television two nights a week, and get to a live card at least once a month. And older fans in those days were disgruntled at *that* amount of action, reminiscing about the decade just past, and the one before that when there was a goddamned live fight card every week, and *good* boxers too.

"People today are not hungry," Leon Grinshpun, formerly

of the Ukraine and the national boxing team of the Soviet Union, was saying to Cooke and me earlier that day over coffee. "In this country kids have it too easy. Who wants to box? They can get welfare."

The same factors have been at work in both the United States and Canada to bring about the decline of boxing but ironically, given the global identification of the sport with the States, the body remained healthier for a decade longer north of the border. But like a guy who smokes three packs of cigarettes a day and washes down his fries and coconut cream pie with a gallon of soft drink, there will be no mystery to the demise. In North America now, the boxing situation provokes the image of a newly dug grave, the headstone freshly carved: "Killed by TV and the good life." The gravediggers are waiting by the piles of dirt, leaning on their shovels; the pallbearers tug their cuffs and check their watches; the heads of all the mourners are bowed in sorrow over the passing of a great hustle. The corpse, however, continues to give a few last twitches.

Up in a heavenly back room, smoky as a cloud, the great Wilson Mizener, manager of the roguish middleweight Stanley Ketchel, has prepared a telegram for the earthly bereaved. He did send it once before, back in the long-gone twenties when Ketchel, "the Michigan Assassin," was himself assassinated by the husband of the young woman with whom he was having breakfast: "Start counting ten and he will get up."

It didn't work then, and it won't work now.

"Every time I get a kid," Leon is saying, "he quits on me. Now I have two young men. All they want to do is get in the ring and throw punches. If they are allowed to do this, it always happens, right away they get hurt, and give up. This is not right. You have to be prepared. You have to be in splendid shape and know the techniques."

Dave nods in agreement. He trains a heavyweight who has had three pro fights. "I never ask a fighter to do any training that I won't do. I'm a forty-three-year-old man; he's a twenty-six-year-old kid. We get halfway through the stomach workout and he remembers he has to be somewhere else."

"Dave, your fighter, tell me if I'm wrong," Leon interjects, "but he relies on raw power; he is not sophisticated."

"He's lazy. He *can* box but he doesn't want to, and how can I make him study defence? His last fight, on the Holyfield-Tillis card, he knocked his opponent out in fifty-two seconds of the first round. So now he thinks he can do the same thing every time out."

"But if you move him up to tougher opponents . . ."

"Which is what I have to do . . ."

" . . . he will find that this does not work, and he will not be prepared. That is when a fighter gets hurt. My fighter, the ideal one I would teach, if he would listen to me, he would not get hurt."

"Mine, he's had three fights. Now he wants $1500 to fight again. Nobody will give that to him."

"Well, they hear all the money that a Sugar Ray Leonard and a Mike Tyson get and they think: 'If they earn millions, I should earn thousands at least.' "

"But I tell him, you get seven or eight big wins in a row, then you can earn $1500, and more. But he doesn't see it that way. He has guts though, this kid; he'll fight anybody as long as the money is right."

"And he will get hurt, and then people will say boxing must be abolished. It is bad."

"I'm not saying he can be heavyweight champion of the world, but if he listened to me, I could get him in the top ten and get him at least one big payday."

"Ah, they don't listen. They don't have heart and hunger."

Leon Grinshpun grew up poor in the Ukraine. A family friend thought the boy could become a good boxer. "In Russia," he says, "every kid goes to camp. Here kids do not have childhoods. In Russia everyone has a wonderful childhood; it is just their adulthood that is no good."

He went to boxing camp after children's camp. "From age fourteen to sixteen, nothing but boxing. I was right away in love with boxing. I was, what you call it, chunky, and always I had good reflexes. Later, they saw that I had patience and might make a good coach. I saw that boxing is not a fight, it is more than a fight. It is art. I studied physical education and specialized in boxing. Is nothing like in Canada. I had years of anatomy, physiology, psychology, biochemistry. Equivalent, I am told, to third year of medical school here.

"In school, I took analytical boxing. Yes. You learn to analyze fighting styles. We even had courses on European, Mexican and American-style boxing. It was taught not only how to fight these ways but how to fight against these styles. So much." Leon divests himself of a mighty shrug and a sigh. "And in Canada, they tell me I don't know how to train boxers!"

After a few years of teaching school and coaching boxing, Grinshpun was given the opportunity to accompany a Russian team to North America as a trainer. He is reluctant to expand upon the events surrounding the journey. Suffice it to say, he became a Canadian. "I landed in Winnipeg and got a job at a slaughterhouse, first day down on the killing floor. I didn't want to do it, all that blood. But I stayed four years. It was hard work but I did it. Why not? It was a job. It did not kill me." He spent his spare time giving boxing lessons at the YMCA. In 1981, he left Winnipeg for Vancouver. The day he arrived, Grinshpun went to the Shamrock Athletic Club on Hastings Street and started coaching boxers. "I got from Ottawa my licence to train amateurs but I gave it up to work with professionals. Olajide Senior asked me to work at his club."

Michael Olajide, called Senior to distinguish him from his son, the former Canadian middleweight champ now fighting out of New York, used to operate a fight club above a store on Main Street in Vancouver. Senior was raised in Nigeria, and turned professional under the tutelage of former lightweight contender Hogan "Kid" Bassey. He emigrated to England, fought for five more years and finally moved to Vancouver. Senior is a short, dark, muscular man given to mercurial changes of mood. A couple of hours into Leon Grinshpun's first day on the job, Senior said, "Well, what do you think of these boys?"

"Okay," Leon shrugged. "Okay."

"Okay? Aren't any of them more than okay?"

"Maybe." Another shrug.

"Who is the best fighter of the bunch?"

Grinshpun looked around, finally pointed to a kid who was in the ring, shadowboxing.

Grinshpun recalls that Senior became agitated and indicated another black kid. "What about him? You think he's any good?"

"No, not very good."

That was the end of Leon's tenure chez Olajide. The second black kid was Michael Junior.

Grinshpun returned to the Shamrock and was training Tony Pep when the six-foot, one-inch featherweight won the Canadian title. In 1986, following a dispute with Pep's manager Tony Dowling, Grinshpun went free-lance for a couple of years until landing a job as fitness instructor and boxing coach at a community centre in the east end of town. "My desire now," he is saying over coffee at the Robson Market, "is to instruct a well-disciplined and hungry young man. The kind, everybody goes to a party, he goes to bed at ten-thirty."

"Lots of luck," says Dave Cooke, smiling at the improbability of it.

"I would like to see somebody who would really work on it. I would teach him the theory and explain *why* you do something, not just how to do it. Defence, I would stress defence like they don't teach here. My fighter would not get hurt like Shawn O'Sullivan did. I would give everything to such a fighter. It would be a pleasure. People would appreciate a boxer like that if they could see one. Ah, good boxing, it is like ballet; it is like chess."

While Grinshpun was growing up in the Ukraine, Dave Cooke was scrabbling on the streets of Vancouver. He was introduced to boxing by an older brother and was thoroughly familiar with the history of the sport before he ever put on the gloves himself, at the relatively late age of twenty-four.

"See, I loved boxing and knew all about it but from the outside. In other words, I didn't really know how it is. How it feels to try to control yourself and defend yourself when your eyes are blurry, your nose is pissing blood and your ears are ringing. They just threw me into the ring right away, and me and another guy started swinging at each other. That's how some of these trainers think. But then Mike Tymal took charge of me, and he taught me the basics. He was a fine, scientific trainer. Now I can not only pass along what I learned from him, I can tell from experience why the scientific approach is better."

Cooke learned his lessons well enough to attract some offers to turn pro. "But I turned them down. I was making good money on the docks, and I knew I had started too late to really be successful. I got enough satisfaction keeping in shape and learning more and more as I went along. I sparred with some pretty good fighters, guys like Yaqui Lopez and Jimmy Young. I guess in the back of my mind, from the beginning, I wanted to be a trainer. My only real success has been training George Jerome when he was managed by Jimmy Johnston. I was in his corner in Toronto when Horst Geisler knocked him out of the ring, and George got back in and knocked Geisler out."

Eventually Cooke and Grinshpun begin to reminisce about the roster of rapscallions with whom they have been involved. These include numerous street punks, bikers, Tough Guy contest contenders, illegal immigrants, starry-eyed kids who quit when they saw stars for real and one three-hundred-pound scion of a Nevada mob family. Despite the futility of having worked with this sorry lot, both men are as anxious as little boys to add another name to the list, a name that would redeem all the frustration and wasted hours. They suddenly start to remind me of Andy Hardy running around the picket-fence neighbourhood with his big idea, and soon they have me tagging along with them. First we would need a clubhouse, a place to train all the future champs, then we'd find the aspirants themselves. We'd have the place going round the clock, a veritable emporium of pugilism. They'd train, I'd manage, staying on the phone to all hours, calling up managers and matchmakers all over the world: "I got a heavyweight with six wins, no losses, and I wanna put him in with a tall guy with a good jab. Need a win though but not too easy. What? Yeah, I can bring along a welter too. He's all right, 6 and 4. Uh huh, passports are in order. Where? The Philippines? Sure. Next week? The tickets will be waiting? Yeah, right. Listen, you'll have a guy there at the airport in Manila, eh? He'll drive us to Quezon City? Okay, you got a deal. See you, pal."

"Yeah," says Dave Cooke, "but where do you *find* these guys?"

"Guys who have heart?" Leon wants to know.

"Well, maybe," says I, "a block from here."

And that is how Dave Cooke and I come to be striding through the lunch-hour crowd to the immigration centre on Alberni Street. Leon stays behind, having had his fill of such places. I have been in the office a few times, circulating among the gangs of people waiting to discuss their applications. They come from every country in the world—and many of them are young and look hungry. Dave stands wide-eyed on the threshold of the big room.

"Look there," I say, "those guys. Central Americans. That one, an Indonesian, I think."

"Yeah, and them." Dave nods his head in the direction of two black guys. "An African would be good."

"So, anyway, you see what I mean?"

"Uh huh. Yeah. I sure do."

"I know a fellow who works here. Sort of like a doorman, tells people what to do. He'll let me come in, circulate among the people. There's a translator here, speaks a dozen languages; he'll help us out."

"Yeah. I'll give you a stack of my cards, and you can pass them out."

We leave, and Dave's walk is now even more animated than usual as he considers the situation out loud. Of course, it might *seem* predatory, but you could look at us as a couple of kids peering in a candy-shop window. Someone of a more cynical nature would smirk and compare us to pimps checking out fresh talent at the bus station. But we are recruiting, that's all; same as a rock group manager visits the bar or an editor peruses the quarterlies. Only, it is true, we are dealing in flesh and blood.

After a couple of blocks, Dave, who must have been listening to himself, says a trifle sheepishly, "This boxing bug, it gets in your blood when you're a kid and it never leaves."

Pals

His first name was Felix. He was the quietest kid in the neighbourhood, and he owned a pair of satin boxing trunks. He was shorter than I was, more compact with what then was considered the perfect build for a future middleweight. All of us kids fought, in the ring and on the streets; it came with the territory, South Philadelphia. But Felix was the real thing.

He had the kind of complexion often called olive, dark blond hair and pale blue-grey eyes; it made for a curious combination.

The satin trunks were crimson with a snow-white waistband and stripe down the hip. All that I remember vividly, but not his last name. He wasn't a part of our gang and I hardly ever saw him although he lived near by, on Ninth Street close to Porter. He was shy but it wasn't that that kept him apart from us, as at first we figured. No, his old man had him on a rigorous schedule.

There was another kid in the neighbourhood, a few years older than us, who also lived on Ninth Street and was a serious boxer. His name I remember well, and not only because I fought him—unwillingly—in a Police Athletic League bout. Ike Beloff. He was touted as a future professional contender and, as a kid of thirteen or fourteen, was already being trained or in other ways tutored by the very good black middleweight Gil Turner.

Beloff had no sense of cool. But Gil Turner was cool, pulling into the white neighbourhood in his white '53 Cadillac, in a sharkskin suit, Ban-Lon shirt underneath like Sugar Ray Robinson.

Big Beloff, as we called him, laid a whipping on me. Actually, the fight didn't last long enough to be considered a whipping. It was my third amateur bout, at the police station at Third and Jackson streets. I'd had my second amateur bout not more than an hour before, and I'd won. Beloff was the biggest kid there, but I had been a wise guy, saying loudly that I didn't think he was so great. So when it was discovered there was no opponent Beloff's size, the boss, having heard my mouthing off, urged me into the ring. I hadn't said *I* could beat him. But I had to go through with it, not because I was afraid of being considered afraid—hell, nobody else wanted to fight him either—but because I didn't want the cop to have one on me. There was a complicated social dynamic in those parts. None of us were suddenly going to metamorphose into choirboys; confrontations with the law were on every kid's horizon. If I backed away from Big Beloff, it would become part of the collective cop consciousness. To wit: "So that punk's in trouble, huh? Well, we know he's really yellow." And they'd make it worse for me. Therefore, in putting on the gloves against Beloff, I was investing in my future. ("Well, at least the kid's no chicken, so we'll go easy on him . . .")

I climbed through the ropes; I circled; he closed and I went down. I took the eight count, but was soon down again. Humiliated now, I lost my temper. Beloff timed a couple of my wild swings, then belted me with a vicious straight right that ended the encounter right there. My nose was sore, my eyes watery. I was disoriented but wanted more. Beyond the referee's shoulder, I could see the old basketball backboard shimmering against the far wall of the gymnasium. Fortunately, the ref permitted no more. There was a round of boos in that musty second-floor hall that Saturday afternoon in 1955, but they were not for me. The crowd did not approve of the hulking Big Beloff grinning, proud of his victory over a kid half his size. My own pals clapped me on the back: "You did good, man. You hit him with a few shots there when you got mad. That punk . . ."

But Beloff somehow was not as impressive as Felix, even though he did eventually get a top ten ranking in days when such a thing meant more than it does now. Felix was cool. Felix was a boxer from the inside out.

Once Felix invited me inside his house. I was the first kid to be so honoured, and the last. Later, the rest of the gang wanted to know all the details: what kind of stuff the family had in there, what the secret was. There had to be some explanation for Felix's mysterious aloofness, and the explanation had to dwell in that red-brick row house. But it was no different from any other Italian working-class house, which meant it was cleaner and neater inside than the corresponding Jewish home or that of any other nationality, I suppose, had there been another nationality represented in that neighbourhood. In the living room where Felix and I stood talking was a white armchair covered with transparent plastic. Felix's mother was framed in the kitchen doorway stirring something at the stove. She had blonde hair. She said hello, did I want anything to eat? The old man came down the stairs and took no notice of me as he barked an order: "Felix, go upstairs and do your sit-ups."

Felix had his own room with a rug on the floor and a rubber exercise mat between the blond wood dresser and the bed. On the dresser and the walls were photographs, some autographed, of well-known Italian fighters like Joey Giardello, Tony DeMarco and Rocky Graziano. Felix got right down onto the mat. "I got to do one-hundred-fifty a day. Same number of push-ups."

The idea of this was incredible to me, and to the guys I reported to later. It was subsequently determined that, although some of us had done a few push-ups, nobody had ever done sit-up number one. We immediately got to it, but nobody could do, or was interested in doing, more than twenty.

As well, Felix ran every morning except Sunday, and did calisthenics every day and ring work every other day. He didn't go to the precinct gym like the rest of us but to a real boxing gym on Moyamensing Avenue.

As I was leaving, Felix said, "Wait. I wanna show you something." From the bottom drawer of the blond dresser, he took a cardboard box, like one from a department store. He opened it, and there were the boxing shorts resting on a bed of tissue paper. He set the box on the bed, the spread pale yellow with tufts that formed flowery swirls. The red satin caught the light through the gauzy window curtain and glittered. "For the Golden Gloves," Felix said. They were beautiful all right, symbolizing all his eager seriousness and promise. They were cool, too.

The rest of us neighbourhood punks, at least the ones who qualified for the PAL team—Eddie Schwartz, Phil Cooper, Ralphie Fortunato and me—made do with cheap gym shorts and sleeveless T-shirts with "38th Precinct" on the front. We had them courtesy of the Bishops, a family who had a little bread from two sons who were making it in show business in the Catskills and Atlantic City.

I boxed in the Police Athletic League for two years until we moved out of the city. There was no real training to speak of and I don't recall getting any personal attention. There was an old cop named Johnny Gambini who sat in a huge chair and shouted orders in loud grunts. He rarely got up from the chair. Once a cop on the beat, Sergeant Gambini was now fat and sick. They had given him this job to take care of him. His son, who had been a PAL boxer, was sick too, dying of leukemia. The sarge just sat there exuding sadness. We tried not to look at him directly but could not help noticing in our peripheral vision the incredible herniated bulge of his testicles. It was like a boxing glove stuck down his pant leg. When he did get up, he walked bent over, huffing, puffing, snuffling through his nose. But mostly I remember him sitting in that wooden chair with the armrests scarred black by cigar butts. In back of him, vertical tongue-and-groove slats rose from the floor for five feet. Above that border, dirty plaster walls that probably once were white. A couple of backboards without hoops. No fight posters, just a ring, an abdominal board with a ripped leather covering, a gymnast's mount that we called a horse, and wide, grey-painted board floors. Later I recognized this place, or a reasonable facsimile, when I saw the movie *Dead End*. It was the place where Pat O'Brien took the delinquents to make good citizens of them.

Now and again Gambini would be moved to lecture. "Youse kids, most of you, youse never had no breaks. Your mothers and fathers they never had no breaks. You got it tough. You come from a tough place."

I didn't realize it was a tough place until I moved out and kids in the suburbs pronounced the words "South Philadelphia" with a mixture of awe and superiority. Even now, a middle-aged man in Canada, I encounter the mythic reputation of

South Philadelphia, mention of it in the newspapers always preceded by "the mean streets of . . ."

Gambini continued by saying that, inasmuch as we were unlucky in this regard, we should be smart and thinking of ways to escape. "All youse kids, youse got a choice. I mean, maybe some of you can sing like Eddie Fisher or Buddy Greco"—neighbourhood touchstones in this pre-rock'n'roll era—"but I doubt it. If you can, good luck to you but if not, what're your choices, huh? You got crime, or you got some job in a warehouse you're looking at. You got another choice. You got boxing." Sergeant Gambini was right about that. But me, I didn't pay much attention. Neither did most of the others. We messed around, singing a cappella outside the luncheonette, but none of us seriously considered a singing career. As for crime, maybe that would come later, but our idea of crime was different too. There was no crime in South Philadelphia except organized crime. A warehouse job? A clerk's job? We were going to be Mickey Mantle, or basketball stars like Bob Cousy, whose book on basketball fundamentals came free with a pair of high-top sneakers. If it wasn't baseball or basketball, it would be some kind of big-shot hustle that would allow us to drive Cadillacs like the one Gil Turner had.

How right the sarge was. When I think of the old neighbourhood, I can name mob figures, singers and fighters, and nobody notable from any other field of endeavour. But mostly there were fighters, going all the way back to Jack O'Brien and including Tommy Loughran, Joey Archer, Joey Giardello, Joe Frazier, Tyrone Everett, Bennie Brisco, Willie "the Worm" Monroe, Jimmy Young, Frank "the Animal" Fletcher, Matthew Saad Muhammad, Jeff Chandler, Meldrick Taylor.

Boxing was all around you. Two males, ten years old or fifty, might greet each other on the corner by putting up their dukes, giving a little head bob, slipping an imaginary punch. It was natural and friendly.

Now, in middle-class neighbourhoods, it is not unusual for

two boys to assume rigid, stylized martial-arts stances when they see each other, flicking out a kick, pivoting and following up with a tense, ready-for-anything pose, one stiff hand by the chin with the other arm extended. It looks so *mean*. The boys always look self-conscious, not to mention awkward.

Inherent in this street-corner, shopping-mall identification with martial arts seems to be the need to glorify the self by wreaking vengeance on another person, or persons. In a young man's boxing fantasies, he wins a tough fight against a worthy opponent, or has to knock the other fellow out before he can display his worthiness. Either way, he is up against one other guy who goes down for the count, not the big sleep. The day-dreams of kick boxers seem to be far darker. Whole squadrons of opponents are maimed or killed, half a dozen squad cars' worth of cops are decimated. It is not Rocky Balboa taking the Russian down to the final round, it's Bruce Lee destroying half of Hong Kong.

Back then it was boxing that was all around you. There was a refinement even in street encounters. Tex Cobb, who went fifteen rounds with Larry Holmes, was quoted as saying that in South Philadelphia, even the winos throw jabs.

Everybody had an uncle or a father who fought. My old man, never a real professional, nevertheless boxed for money in smokers and bouts organized in playgrounds or back rooms, wherever there was enough space to set up a ring or mark off a sixteen-to-twenty-foot square. The details of his seesaw battle with Billy Winston, "a good-looking coloured boy and good friend," are vivid in my mind. The match was held on the hardwood floor at the settlement house at Fifth and Christian streets. "I got a decision—it was close, though": so the legend went.

The neighbourhoods were filled with fighters. Uncle Joe and Aunt Lena had a luncheonette at Fifth and Catherine where I hung around. My old man or somebody else would point to some character and say, "See that guy? Used to be a pretty good welterweight in his day." Or, "That man there? He fought Dempsey." That man there was named Joe Grimm. I remember him as big and old, reaching down into the soda tub, his huge hairy hand coming up with water running off it, holding a bottle. This was in the early fifties, so his bout with Dempsey would have been thirty years past. My father and I used to watch "Greatest Fights of the Century" on TV, so I saw Dempsey, "the Manassa Mauler," bombing Luis Firpo, standing over him and clubbing him down again as soon as he got up. Saw Dempsey destroy "the Ambling Alp," Primo Carnera. So in the luncheonette, I leaned against the pinball machine looking at this old Joe Grimm, at his dripping hand, the hand that hit Dempsey.

There was a distant relative named Joey Foglietta who'd been a successful amateur but a failure as a pro. I'd see him around the Ninth Street market, punchy, a stereotype, mumbling to himself, shrugging his shoulders and snorting through a twisted nose. On the other hand, unmarked after two hundred bouts was my father's uncle, Andy Juliano. He'd fought as a lightweight under the name Andy Kolb. A sharp dresser, a tough, tender little man with glasses and slicked-back hair, he once showed me his scrapbooks with clippings of bouts dating from the bare-knuckle era. Once, crossing the Passyunk Avenue bridge on his way home from a match, Uncle Andy heard someone in the water screaming for help and dove in to save him. I remember part of the headline on the story: "Fighting Hero Dives from Bridge . . . " Three years before he died at age eighty-eight, Uncle Andy was in his yellow Corvair convertible at a traffic light on Moyamensing Avenue when two hoods jumped him. He laid both of them out with a tire iron.

But boxing remained remote from our imaginative lives. Since it was in the atmosphere, we knew all too well the discipline and pain it involved. Even if, lying in bed on a Friday night, having just seen some thrilling television fight brought to you by Gillette ("To look sharp and be on the ball"), maybe

Yvon Durelle-Archie Moore, the Fighting Fisherman knocking the Mongoose down four times in the first round yet failing to finish him off—even if you might dream of stepping in for Durelle and beating Moore, you knew you'd have to pay a big price to get there, and it would cost much more to stay there until, inevitably, you would be replaced. To make any money after beating aging Archie in '54, you'd have to move up to heavyweight and take on Marciano, "the Brockton Blockbuster." Who could forget the photograph of Jersey Joe Walcott's face distorted into ogre shape by a right from the Rock? Even the most modest childhood boxing fantasy was undercut with agony and seriousness.

Instead, we all dreamed of baseball stardom. Me, I roamed centre field making Willie Mays basket catches, rolled up my T-shirt sleeves like Ted Kluzewski, assumed Stan Musial's question-mark batting stance. Boxing was all around, but major-league baseball took place in a magic realm high above and far away from the red-brick row-house streets. The actual concrete stadium was there at Twenty-first and Lehigh. You passed through those portals, and as you climbed the steps got that first magic glimpse of ballpark blue sky, then the tops of the bleachers opposite, the centre field wall with the 421-feet sign, the thrilling green grass and red-gold infield dirt. The players themselves were impossibly heroic, all of them, not just Mantle and Mays, Ted Williams and Duke Snider, but Smokey Burgess and Gus Zernial as well. They occupied a region apart from the world of ordinary men, far beyond fathers and uncles, and this was the sphere to which we aspired, a place we allowed ourselves to truly believe we could attain.

Not one of us could name a major-league baseball player who hailed from South Philadelphia, or any place in Philadelphia, for that matter. But the power of the dream was so strong that the practicality of not even having a proper place to practise real baseball never intruded. There was a hard-packed dirt playing field at Third and Oregon avenues, six blocks away, and every

Saturday morning we set out on the major expedition necessary to get there. The getting there entailed fighting, as did the staying and playing. We felt like cavalry scouts heading out into Indian territory. We had to pass through two distinct black neighbourhoods and the kids would be waiting for us with fists, rocks, chains and brass knuckles. First the Apaches and then the Pawnees, is the way we thought of it. After all that, we'd have to fight to get a place on the field. Once we had attained the field, we were entitled by general consensus to an hour and a half's play, but we often had to confront outlanders who didn't respect this agreement. The result of all this struggling was that we played hard like Ty Cobb and Pistol Pete Reiser; there was not a George Bell among us.

At some point, this dream faded or was traded in for more modest grown-up hopes and expectations. But it is the foundation of all baseball writing, both its strength and its weakness. Almost tactile is the nostalgia, yet writers get away with it, whether in *The New Yorker* or *Baseball Digest*, because it is an assertion of childhood, theirs and, by extension, everyone else's. There is an article that turns up several times a year in American publications wherein a middle-aged man with a paunch, a receding hairline and a fungo bat is hitting them out to his ten-year-old son. The bat becomes a magic wand melding two childhoods in a timeless continuum. The sand-lot experience is a device used to cross the threshold—the literary threshold, anyway—of one of life's big moments. Dear old Dad faces the fact that he can no longer hit them out of sight like he used to do (or likes to think that he used to do) on those diamonds of the halcyon past. His path around the bases eventually leads to home and the intractable catcher, and Dad is left at the plate swinging too late his mortal ash at the grim reaper's high hard one. Not that they ever *write* that; it is all supposed to be bittersweetly understood by the reader as the father walks, arm over the kid's shoulder, off the field.

Commentators who do not understand boxing—Ernest

Hemingway, for instance—have seen it as a metaphor for life. Boxing is not like life, although life, as Joyce Carol Oates has said, is often like boxing. Baseball makes a much better metaphor: all those boring stretches while the batter fouls off eleven straight pitches and you wait, spitting between your shoes, out in left field. What transpires in the ring is never boring. Every punch thrown and received wears down the fighter, and, thus, the wonder of his skill is being destroyed irrevocably at the moment it is displayed. This awful drama, played out in a ring where death lurks invisible but felt, peering between the ropes, is of religious import. Boxing is not *like* religion; in a very real and pagan sense, it *is* religion. Boxers, referee, seconds, judges, timekeepers and spectators are all participants in an invocation of the spirits, calling forth those nameless gods while simultaneously presenting themselves for approval, rejection, acknowledgement. The entire spectacle is a ghost dance around an eerie fire in hyper-reality, a ritualistic performance consuming itself in flames.

But such therianthropic lucubrations are part of prize fighting and later years. In a fifties baseball childhood, the sun shone on green grass and a golden infield, and there were no night games. Boxing was something to fool around with and watch on television. That beyond the ropes wherein those rascals battled were even greater rascals machinating all over the place, with no restraints whatsoever, was to me a notion more remote than even metaphysics.

Mugs, Pugs, Thugs and Dreamers

There were "Wednesday Night Fights" and "Friday Night Fights," as well as the "Greatest Fights of the Century" and special events like the Louis-Marciano bout. Usually I watched these on television with my father at our second-floor apartment on Seventh and Catherine streets. "He should have never done it," the old man said, as Louis lay on the canvas in the eighth round, referee Ruby Goldstein counting him out. "Come out of retirement. But he's in debt real bad. His manager stole all his money and he has to pay a lot of income tax to the government."

Throughout my childhood, I never heard the name Joe Louis without an accompanying line about his financial predicament. The picture that emerged was of a trusting but dimwitted sharecropper's son who, although attaining the heavyweight championship, was victimized by unscrupulous handlers and reduced to making a pathetic comeback attempt against the Rock. Later Louis suffered even greater ignominy as a wrestler, forever hounded by income tax guys who probably looked like Jack Webb and Ben Alexander on "Dragnet," who were relentless and never smiled.

In 1935, one Mike Jacobs had taken over the promotion of Joe Louis. In 1988, Marty Cohen, ninety-two-year-old vice-president of the World Boxing Council, remembered Jacobs as "the most ferocious hustler in boxing history." Jacobs started out as a "digger," buying theatre and opera tickets for scalpers. By the age of thirteen, he had gone into business for himself, saving enough money in three years to buy the refreshment concession on the Battery Park-Coney Island ferry. A free lunch was included in the price of a boat ticket, so Jacobs had to innovate to turn a decent profit. The salted peanuts he sold cheap led to a thirsty demand for his expensive lemonade. Then there was his candy hustle. Jacobs made two laps of the boat deck, the first to give candy to any young woman on a date; on the second, he asked payment for what the couple had assumed was free. Most gentlemen, fearing a scene with Jacobs or being thought cheap by their girls, paid up. Jacobs waited on tables at Tamany Hall during the off-season but devoted most of his time to ticket scalping. He arranged tours for Enrico Caruso and British suffragette Emmeline Pankhurst. During the First World War, he secured the refreshment concessions for a number of army camps but sold out before the armistice. He got involved in boxing in 1916, lending money to Tex Rickard to stage the Willard-Moran heavyweight bout in exchange for a healthy number of tickets to scalp. Later, he worked out of a small office at Madison Square Garden advising Rickard, who was the garden's promoter. When Rickard died in 1929, Jimmy Johnston, a boxing hustler known as "the boy bandit," rather than Jacobs, was named his successor. Jacobs dedicated himself to taking revenge on the garden and found his vehicle in the milk fund charity sponsored by Mrs. William Randolph Hearst.

Marty Cohen, at the time putting on fights at the St. Nicholas Arena, remembers this scam well. "The idea was for the garden to host these boxing shows, a percentage of the profit going to the Hearst Milk Fund. The shows themselves were promoted by Damon Runyon and two other Hearst writers, Bill Farnsworth and Eddie Frayne. But the garden got greedy and so, in turn, did Runyon and his pals. When the garden raised the rent, Runyon saw his chance. The writers formed the Twentieth Century Boxing Club but they couldn't have stock in their names since they wanted to tout the shows in their columns. Enter Mike. He took over running the Milk Fund shows from the garden and from Jimmy Johnston. The writers insured their success and Mrs. Hearst got her milk money."

Jacobs again bested Johnston and broke the garden's monopoly on big-time boxing when he assumed promotion of the up-and-coming Joe Louis. Johnston had been offered a chance at Louis, but had told one of the Brown Bomber's black managers over the phone that "the nigger will have to lose a few to white boys if he wants a chance at the title." In stepped Jacobs. As Louis said later, "Mike had no prejudice over a man's colour if the man could make a green buck for him."

He who controls the heavyweight champion of the world controls boxing: the adage was as true then as it is now. And Jacobs saw no reason to share his power with a trio of sports scribes. Not long after Louis beat Jimmy Braddock for the championship, the Hearst company combined its two New

York papers, the *Journal* and the *American*. Frayne got the job as sports editor but Farnsworth was let go. Jacobs gave him a job but demeaned the ex-reporter, making him open mail and fetch coffee. When Farnsworth could take it no longer, he quit and, needing money, sold his shares in the Twentieth Century Boxing Club to Jacobs. Next, Jacobs gave the story of the writers' collusion in Twentieth Century to the competing *World Telegram*, a Scripps-Howard paper. The Hearst Corporation could not allow its objectivity to be compromised by such a conflict of interest, and ordered Runyon and Frayne to dispose of their interests in Twentieth Century. Jacobs purchased their shares cheap, at $25,000 to a man.

But my father and the rest of them were wrong about the compulsive hustler robbing Joe Louis. Jacobs billed the Brown Bomber as an ambassador between the races, a black man no white man need fear unless he stepped into the ring with him. Jacobs made Louis rich and himself rich, and if Louis didn't stay that way it wasn't entirely Jacobs's fault. All he did was give Louis money when the boxer asked for it. The worst that could be said of Jacobs was that he was like the company store, and every day Joe Louis got another day older and deeper in debt.

Louis had to pay his debt to Jacobs before he collected any money for a fight. Then there was the manager's standard one-third cut plus expenses. Next came the trainer's 10 per cent. Louis got what was left over. Louis's purse for his 1946 fight with Tammy Muriello was $100,000. A month after the bout, the champ was down to his last five hundred bucks. Forty thousand was invested in a Chicago night spot called the Rumboogie Club that folded overnight, its owners suddenly nowhere to be found. There was the Champ's entourage to be taken care of, and when you travelled with the Champ, you travelled first-class. Louis went to his manager, begging for a loan. "Jeez, Joe. What's the matter?" Jacobs asked. "How come you still got five hundred left?"

There just never seemed enough to give any of it to the IRS.

Boxing is like the old shell game: the pea is not under the one you thought it was under even though you *saw* it there. Watching a fight promoter is like watching a three-card monte dealer. Unless you accept the fact that the con is on, you are fooling yourself.

Unlike other major sports, boxing is not and never has been run by individuals who could be mistaken for pillars of any community other than their own. While Supreme Court justices, corporate miracle workers and Ivy League university presidents have been chosen for top positions in the baseball world, mobsters, ex-numbers runners and worse have clawed their way to the top of the boxing heap. You need know nothing of former baseball commissioners Kenesaw Mountain Landis, Peter Uberroth or A. Bartlett Giametti; their names tell who they were, as do the monikers of boxing's former lords: Blinky Palermo, Frankie Carbo, Big Jim Norris. The first name of baseball's current commissioner is Fay. It is unthinkable that anyone with a name like that could even get close to boxing. Boxing is not an establishment sport; it is a monument to anarchism. Crooked? Well, as the police chief said to the reporters at the beginning of the novel *Asphalt Jungle*, "You guys are always complaining that boxing is corrupt. Well, let me ask you something: compared to *what*?"

Compared to the machinations of today's big-time boxing promoters, the antics of the old guard seem almost quaint. With those guys there was a human touch, if only the touch of human behinds stuck to Tex Rickard's uncured pine bleachers. Once boxing was controlled by riverboat gamblers and ticket scalpers; it has, for the past twenty years, been in the hands of a Harvard Law School graduate and a guy who did a nickel for manslaughter. The only thing Bob Arum and Don King have in common, besides mutual antipathy, is a predilection, when all other defences have been exhausted, for falling back on the charge of prejudice, as in, "If I wasn't Jewish you wouldn't hear that kind of stuff about me," and "They think they can say that about me because I'm a black man." Ironically, both have made fortunes in the WASP world of television sports.

Born in 1932 and raised in New York, Arum got his introduction to boxing while working on Wall Street. Employed by the tax division of the U.S. attorney general's office, he had to examine the closed-circuit revenues from the Sonny Liston-Floyd Patterson fight in 1962. Arum didn't know from boxing, but he knew figures. Three years later, he managed an introduction to the current heavyweight champion, Muhammad Ali. The champ's original Louisville syndicate of backers broke up, and Arum formed Top Rank Incorporated to promote Ali's fights. When the government stripped Ali of his crown for refusing induction into the army, Arum staged an elimination tournament to find a new heavyweight champion. When Ali returned in 1970, it was with Arum as his lawyer and closed-circuit promoter.

Guys like Rickard and Jacobs borrowed or even put up their own money to promote a fight. Arum was the first to package the entire enterprise. His first big score was Leonard-Duran I, which grossed over $30 million. In recent years he has put together Hagler-Hearns and Leonard-Hagler, and packaged weekly fight cards for Top Rank Boxing on the cable network ESPN.

Arum is the man television executives and guys wanting a closed-circuit franchise are most comfortable dealing with. He's a white college graduate, one who says, "I'm a businessman. Two guys fighting in a ring, that has nothing to do with me. Fighters bore me." When pressed on this attitude, Arum responds with a brilliant display of his style: "Look, fighters are getting ripped off worse than they ever were in the Frankie Carbo gangster days. You have to have an absolute line of demarcation between the promoter and the manager. The manager must be on the side of the fighter, and he must battle the promoter for the most possible money. They have to be independent. More and more, they're not. More and more a father like Don King operates through a front like his son."

People around boxing have a tendency not to say nice things about Bob Arum unless they are currently working with him. Bob Waters, a columnist for Long Island's *Newsday*, wrote, "I was talking with Bob Arum. He told me something and I said, 'But Bob, yesterday you told me the exact opposite.' Arum answered, 'I know. Today I'm telling you the truth, yesterday I was lying.' " The British promoter Mickey Duff says, "I'll shake hands with Arum but I'll take my ring off first." The late Cus D'Amato, who rescued Mike Tyson from the streets as he had Floyd Patterson three decades earlier, maintained that Bob Arum "is one of the worst people in the western hemisphere. I don't know the eastern hemisphere very well, but I suspect he'd be one of the worst people there too if he went there." "The master of all evil," Don King calls his rival, "a despicable and unconscionable cad."

Amidst the metaphoric verbiage directed at Arum, the words of Toronto fight manager Ray Rutter seem exotic for their sobriety. Although Rutter, who manages Nedrie Simmons and Willie Featherstone, has conferred with Arum, he has not benefited materially from the contact. "Sharpest guy I ever had to deal with in promotions. I spent two-and-a-half hours with him when he was supposed to promote the Featherstone-Hill fight. He flew up to Toronto. I said, 'Bob, I'll tell you straight out. In a way, I'm out of my league and you're holding all the cards. I'll tell you what I require for Willie's services. I'm going to be honest with you and I expect you to be honest with me.' And he was. We've talked a number of times since. He even calls me now, asks about this guy or that one. He's given me opportunities, but some of them, I've had to say, 'Bob, I don't want to get involved with these guys, they're bad bastards.' As for Don King, I've never dealt with him and I don't intend to."

Don King and his five brothers and sisters were raised by their mother after their father was killed in an industrial accident. In 1951, at the age of nineteen, King got into the numbers racket and went straight to the top. "They called me Kingpin and the Numbers Czar and Donald the Kid King. I was good," he told an interviewer. He claims that numbers was good training for his future line of work. "You have to do most of it out of your head, always be on the run and still come out with a profit. I had to establish liaisons, same as I do now in boxing."

One of those liaisons was with an ex-con named Sam Garrett. King took bets and kept as many as he could cover, laying off the rest with others, one of whom was Garrett. One day Garrett supposedly held back on his payment to King. Garrett claimed he hadn't been able to lay off the lucky number but King accused him of keeping the money the number brought in. King says he told Garrett, "I just ain't gonna play with you no more," and turned to walk away. "When I was getting in the Cadillac, he challenged me from behind. And in the kicking and fighting of what I call the frustrations of the ghetto expressing themselves, this man's head hit the concrete. Seven, eight days later, he expired." King is six feet, two inches tall and in the numbers days weighed two hundred pounds (compared to his present two-fifty). Garrett was five-six and one hundred and thirty-five pounds. Convicted of second-degree murder, King served four years in the Marion Correctional Institute and was released in September 1971. He is fond of saying that jail was his school. At other times, he maintains he matriculated on the streets. The truth is that he acquired a variegated education. He read Aristotle and Homer and "got into Sigmund Freud." But his main man was William Shakespeare. "Man, I love Bill Shakespeare. He was some bad dude."

King made time serve him, and when he got back to the streets he was ready for boxing. He hired fighter-turned-trainer Richie Giachetti to act as a sort of guide through the Byzantine fight world. King's first move was to purchase the contract of heavyweight Earnie Shavers. In early 1974, he was hired by Video Techniques, a closed-circuit firm, to be a consultant for the Foreman-Norton championship bout. Later that same year,

Shavers was knocked out by Jerry Quarry and King had his first contretemps with Bob Arum. The latter seized Shavers's purse in order to guarantee that Arum would receive the $4000 due him from closed-circuit rights in Ohio. "I felt emasculated," King recalls. "The man didn't even give me a chance to pay him." A month later, Arum allegedly reneged on his promise to grant King closed-circuit rights for the second Ali-Frazier fight. But King would soon have his revenge. He put together the Foreman-Ali fight in Zaire—the Rumble in the Jungle—pulling it off right under the nose of Bob Arum. With a heavyweight championship under his belt, King was on his way. There followed several more Ali bouts, including the third fight with Frazier, the Thrilla in Manila.

He may often come on like Don King Kong in pimp threads, but in negotiations King is quiet and careful, and he works harder than anyone else. Mort Sharnik, formerly of "CBS Sports," says, "You call Don King at midnight, tell him a fighter is ready to sign, and he'll be on a plane by 1:00 A.M. He'll get there by 6:00 A.M., sign the papers, be half-dead and someone will say, 'Don, so-and-so just called; he's ready to do business.' And before you can turn around, Don will be off and running again."

Whereas Arum is reputed to be a liar who screws people for the hell of it, King employs other methods. Fighters and managers maintain that King will sign them for a certain amount, make the fight, and then, just as it is about to happen, say that something else has come up, something totally unforeseen. To cover it, King says, the fighter's purse will have to be cut in half. Manager and fighter are therefore left with a take-it-or-leave-it situation. Most of them take it, there being no alternative. A contractual conundrum of the Don King variety was faced in 1908 by Tommy Burns, the only Canadian to be heavyweight champion of the world. What he said of promoter J. D. "Huge Deal" MacIntosh fits Don King like an Everlast glove: He may screw you but you'll get kissed a little along the way—and he'll have the option to do it a few more times. No one has described the Don King situation better than Richie Giachetti. "Don King is a liar and a thief, the greediest bastard I've ever known. This guy wants all the money and all the fighters. He talks about fairness and equality, but he wants everything for himself, and doesn't want to give anything to anybody. I spent years hoping Don would change. He didn't and he won't. The man's greatest asset is that he was born black, because the fighters are black. He knows them. He knows how to rile them, how to sweet-talk them. He'll say and do whatever it takes to win them over. And all the while the man's so insecure he goes around wearing his hair like a fucking idiot so people will recognize him. If I was a fighter and needed a promoter, who would I take? Don King. The man is the best. Don King delivers."

There are other big promoters in the States besides King and Arum, Butch Lewis, Lou Duva and Josephine Abercrombie being chief among them. But Don King is at the top and the big reason he delivers is that he holds all the options, literally and figuratively. When he signs a fighter, he takes options on the fighter's next few bouts. It is not unusual for King to hold promotional rights to both fighters in a given contest. When King was starting out, he arranged a meeting through Cleveland promoter Don Elbaum with heavyweight champion Joe Frazier. Elbaum recalls watching the Frazier-Foreman match on television at home in Cleveland. "I see King coming up to the ring with Frazier's guys." Then Foreman stunned the boxing world by knocking Frazier down six times before the fight was stopped in the second round. "I'm looking at the screen," Elbaum says, "and they're showing all the guys going crazy in Foreman's corner, and there's King right in the middle of it. I said to myself, 'You got to watch out for this guy.' "

Rile, sweet-talk, wheedle or cajole, Don King will do what he thinks necessary. Britain's Mickey Duff, who managed the very fine middleweight John "the Beast" Mugabi, sent his fighter to the States to fight Curtis Ramsey. Duff usually accompanied his Ugandan fighter everywhere but couldn't this time due to a family emergency. Mugabi went with trainer George Francis, who was under instructions to call Duff in England as soon as the fight was over. Duff was sitting in his living room, "biting my nails," when Francis called with the news that Mugabi had knocked Ramsey out in the second round. "Then Don King gets on the phone and says, 'Mickey, the kid's good but we got a problem. He's begging me to take over his career. He says he wants Don King to run him, but I told him no. I said you and I are friends, Mickey, and I won't take him on unless he lets me keep you as a fifty-fifty partner.' "

"Don," said Duff, "I didn't know you speak Swahili."

"I don't," King answered.

"That's interesting, because Mugabi doesn't speak a word of English."

It is an axiom of the sweet science: you have a fighter, someone is going to try and get him from you.

Bob Arum has called for a clear line of demarcation between manager and promoter. Sounds like a good idea, although you have to wonder whether it is aimed at preventing irregularities or at Don King and his son Carl. If allowed to put the package together while guiding the career of one of the fighters, the promoter will obviously have the opportunity to slight the fighter he is not managing. Some sanctioning bodies make a pretext of requiring that there be an actual manager whose name is not the same as that of the promoter. But since boxing generally cannot be governed the particulars easily avoid policing. There is no lime-outlined rectangle for the manager to stay inside like a third-base coach. Most managers need to function as promoters at some time or another. You may find yourself the manager of a would-be boxer living in an area that doesn't know boxing, and doesn't want to know. Or your charge may be possessed of incredible potential, yet the two of you are thwarted by a dearth of live bodies upon which to build a record. To get the kid fights you have to *make* the fights. The Kings, the Duvas and the Duffs have done this, as have the Rutters, the Olajides and the Ungermans. A good manager's job is to promote his boy, just as a promoter must be interested in how fighters' careers and reputations are managed.

And, of course, the promoter of record may not be the actual promoter. There may be a money man seeking profit but wishing to remain silent behind a corporate identity. Or the man putting up the money may be content to keep his hands off the promotion in exchange for the vicarious thrill of the action and the reflected glow of the fight mob.

An Arum, a King or an unknown local may bring together the principals, make the deal and finagle the vigorish, but they do not actually make the event happen. This is the responsibility of the on-site promoters, the Vince Giantomasis of the fight world, who must see that the boxers' medicals are in order, that the judge flying in from Bangkok gets his ticket in time, that requests for press credentials have been properly screened and there is a Fax machine at media headquarters. And those two kids fighting after the main event: Are their records really as presented? What about the challenger's three sparring partners held up at Najarita because of problems with their visas?

If the mythology of baseball is rooted in the dreams of children, boxing is where adults dream. Pity the poor manager. Nowhere is the subconscious more fertile, or febrile, than in the mind of this irrepressible individual. For every cigar-chomping conniver of the cinematic variety, there are a thousand guys in towns from Marleybone to Mbabane who pinch pennies to bring along some kid in whom they have seen just a hint of possibility. An eighteen-year-old boy may be crossing a street in Anyplace and by a deft, graceful side step avoid being hit by a truck. A middle-aged man nearby sees the move and, in the flash of the moment, glimpses outrageous possibilities. He approaches the kid and starts a conversation, assuring him first of all that he is not gay, a nut case or anything on that order, and proceeds to lay out an entire improvised scenario. If the kid is interested, the would-be manager's next step is dinner with Mom and Dad. His head now filled with the same dream, the kid accepts the fact that he is going to have to start getting up at six o'clock to run before going to work in the stock department; maybe it's a job that the manager himself has arranged. After work, there is the workout. The boy may have raw talent but so do thousands of others. In the beginning, the manager himself may teach the fundamentals, rearranging his own schedule and taking time away from his family, but later, when the kid shows progress, a real trainer has to be brought in. Months go by, with the manager paying the trainer and buying the kid's equipment. After a year, there is the first four-round fight, for which the kid earns $250. The manager doesn't have the heart to take his cut. Hell, if the manager abided by the letter of the contract, the young fighter wouldn't see a penny for years. Ray Rutter managed Willie Featherstone for six years before he saw any money from the relationship. After Willie challenged for Virgil Hill's World Boxing Association light heavyweight championship, he had to insist that Rutter take a share.

The heat is always on the manager, and few in Canada draw more of it than Vancouver's Tony Dowling, who has guided the careers of Gordy Racette, Jamey Ollenberger and Tony Pep. "Dowling doesn't mind one of his fighters getting beat as long as he gets his percentage"—so goes the talk.

"Look, I've heard what they say about me, and about other managers," Dowling replies. "But I'll tell you something: me and other guys, we absorb a lot of expenses people don't know about. For instance, not too long ago I sent Tony Pep to train in Miami for three weeks. I paid for the tickets and for his stay. You think I get that back? No way. And no one ever mentions that a manager has to be father, mother, adviser and baby sitter. They don't say anything about the phone calls that come at three in the morning. I don't get paid for any of that. If I did, I wouldn't be looking for work myself."

But the dream endures, and things work according to plan. The fighter progresses undefeated through the four-rounders, the six-round fights and the eights. Then he scores a fourth-round knockout in the first bout scheduled for ten. Afterwards, he says to his manager, "Look, a guy made me an offer I can't refuse. This guy says he has the contacts to move me and you don't. If I want to make something of myself, I have to go with him. You understand what I'm saying?"

Knowing the truth of it, what can the manager do? He has to let the boy go. If the other manager is an honest sort, he will buy out the contract, probably for a pittance. If not, he will just take the kid, knowing that the original manager doesn't have the money it would take to contest the matter in court, nor the ill will to hold up the boy's career. If this picture unfolds in Canada, it takes a more melancholy turn because a good fighter has to go south of the border and the guy waiting to take him over "has contacts in the States."

A few years ago my friend Leon Grinshpun came to me with the story of a Brazilian woman who knew this kid from the São Paulo slums who wanted to be a fighter. Leon wondered whether we should take a look at him. We did, and he showed promise. The plan was that Leon would train and I would manage. We agreed not to display the boy to the fight crowd until he had learned the basics. The kid was talented and had a good story, having come to Canada overland from São Paulo accompanied by a buddy who was dying of a bone marrow disease. He wanted to become a fighter to earn money for his pal's medical care. The big day arrived and we took the kid to the boxing gym in the basement of the Indian Centre on East Hastings Street in Vancouver. Upon his appearance the rhythm of the speed bag was stilled. The fighters stopped working, the trainers, managers and hangers-on ceased talking, and all eyes went to the young man as he mounted the steps to the ring. It reminded me of the new girl strutting her stuff along the main stem for the first time; the fighters were like her competition but the managers were the street-corner pimps, and I wondered who would be the first of them to lay on the words, the equivalent of, "Hey, baby. I'll take *good* care of you, you work for me."

Nobody did steal the Brazilian as it turns out, but nobody had the chance. He was an illegal immigrant and had to disappear suddenly. The experience didn't cost me much but Leon had invested many hours of his time.

Boxing happens in a place you can't hardly get to from suburbia and when you find the ring you've only found a very small part of it. Former heavyweight champion George Foreman said that boxing is like jazz in that only a minuscule portion of the audience knows what is going on. For every move in the ring there is a countermove. Outside that circle, there are literally no rules at all. You want to do boxing business, throw away your MBA and take a course in cigar smoke and mirrors. Hell, when the bell rings, the most interesting stuff has usually happened already. As Barney Nagler and Teddy Brenner say in their book, "Only the ring is square."

"You'll Be All Right, Kid"

Although raised in an atmosphere of prize fighting, I had, apart from smokers, seen only two pro bouts before moving to Canada at age twenty-three. My view of these was limited by my having been a participant in both. Not all fight managers are paragons or cockamamie dreamers, I discovered. Some of these unscrupulous characters will throw an inexperienced, totally unprepared kid—like I was—into a prize ring in front of hundreds of screaming maniacs to possibly get his brains beaten in.

The guy will do this so that he can take one-third of a $250 purse, then try to weasel an additional 10 per cent as a trainer's fee, despite the fact that the only guidance he provided was a hasty, "You'll be all right, kid."

Fresh out of high school, I had travelled down to Virginia on a deal that didn't work out, and found myself living in a room in my aunt's house in Petersburg and working in A. B. Ford's Amoco station outside the Fort Lee Army Base. It was strictly dullsville; the only thing that happened the first month was that I found Bob Dylan's recent, and first, album in the remainder bin of a department store at the Walnut Hill Mall.

I was a sort of juvenile delinquent on the cusp of beatnik hipsterism. During the day I pumped gas and worked on a '48 Hudson I'd bought for thirty-five dollars. At night I read—much Somerset Maugham, of all things—and listened to Bob Dylan. One evening I drove around listening to the CBC broadcast of the Liston-Patterson fight, and came away thinking how much more outspoken Canadian announcers were.

Out of boredom, I signed up for a swimming course at the Petersburg YMCA. Growing up in Philadelphia, the closest we got to swimming was when we opened the fire hydrants on summer evenings. We may have resembled the Dead End Kids but we had no East River to jump into.

One evening after class I went upstairs to the gym and saw two guys working out with gloves on while other kids watched. One boy had a serious outfit, including real flat-heeled boxing shoes and a leather cup worn outside his trunks. The other wore sneakers. I watched a couple of rounds from a distance. A middle-aged fellow came on the scene, shouted pointers to the main boy, and tended the stopwatch. At the end of three rounds, the man said, "Anyone else?" and looked at the boys in turn. Finding no takers, he widened his gaze and spotted me outside the circle. "How 'bout you, pal?" he called.

He put the gloves on me, the leather inside cracked and

sweaty. I went a couple of rounds with the kid and didn't think much of the experience. My nose felt a little funny, that was all. As he was pulling off the gloves, the guy, his name was Guy, said, "You've done this before, huh?"

"Well, I, uh, you know . . ."

"Yeah, I can tell. Tell you what, you want to come by again tomorrow same time, I'll spring for dinner after. Floyd here needs sparring partners. He's got a fight coming up in Norfolk, coupla weeks. His second pro fight."

I started falling by every afternoon. It was something to do and free dinner every night. Once Guy even slipped me a fin. It was true I'd had the gloves on before but not since those Police Athletic League contests, and no one had ever given me any instructions. Still, I had watched enough fights on TV to have a basic idea of what was going on. I possessed a rudimentary knowledge of the proper stance and of balance; knew enough to turn the hand when throwing the jab, and, theoretically, how the straight right and the left hook were to be thrown.

Launching the punches, initiating the attack, is the easy part. Defending yourself is where real skill enters into the game. And with counterpunching, and thinking, you move into another realm. This is where boxing truly becomes art. When you get hit, you have to react like a fighter rather than an ordinary threatened mortal. This response is a learned one, the result of hours in the gym. I suppose it is like going to boot camp, where they break down your personality and remould you into a soldier. A good trainer will break down your street reactions and replace them with those of a prize fighter. Your "natural" reaction must, therefore—ironically—be an "unnatural" reflex. Furthermore, a fighter has to learn to *think*. Get the other guy to make the move you want him to make, so you can make the one you want to make. You have to know the countermoves for everything your opponent may do. It takes hours and hours of sparring, round after round of real boxing to acquire this ability. I had no instruction, few hours invested in trying to employ what I had learned, no ring experience. Luckily for me, this Floyd wasn't much.

Wednesday night, a week or so later, Guy said to me, "Look, boy. I got a call from the people in Norfolk. They got a spot on the card for a middleweight. I told them I had me a boy had a coupla fights up north. What d'you say?"

"Me?"

He wheedled and finagled and finally talked me into it. Luckily, he'd put it to me on a Wednesday rather than, say, a Monday, because then I would have had more time to fret. Back in my room that night, I began pondering the part where he told the fellow I'd had a couple of fights up north. Why make up a story like that? His own boy was on record as having only one fight, so why lie about me? Why not tell the truth, that it was a pro debut? Pro debuts created more interest than bouts between guys with two or three fights. I poked around for hidden meanings like a pig after truffles. I tossed and turned and came up with what had to be the truth. The other boy must be some sort of veteran and to avoid accusations of a gross mismatch my "manager" felt it incumbent upon himself to tell a fib.

Thursday, when I mentioned it, he said, "Not to worry. The coloured boy's had, uh, four fights but he ain't nothing. You'll do fine."

"What about the licence?"

"Everything is all taken care of. All you got to worry about is fighting."

I got Friday and Saturday off work, and the three of us left for Norfolk, travelling down old Highway 460 through tobacco country and peanut fields. Here and there we saw a sawmill or a tin-roof shack propped up at the corners by bricks, hound dogs sleeping under the porch. All the way down, Floyd talked about how his opponent was going to be lucky to survive.

The fights were inside the naval base. My man said, "Oh,

yeah. Listen, boy. You are supposed to be Gary Mason, understand? He couldn't make it down from Baltimore but nobody got to know that." My spirits plunged even further upon discovering that Floyd, rather than me, was on the bottom of the card. This meant my midnight speculations had been correct. I was the third fight, which indicated that I was supposed to have some experience. As it turned out, Gary Mason was 3 and 0; his opponent—*my* opponent—Lanny Jansen was 4 and 1.

There were eight fights on the card. The bottom ten fighters split two washrooms and the top six had other facilities. Opponents were separated. You changed your clothes and stored them in the toilet stalls and sat in there if you wanted to sit, or leaned against the sinks, paced, or moved around throwing punches. My man left with Floyd, and when the door opened I heard the noise of the crowd. There had only been a few people out there earlier; now it sounded like Madison Square Garden for Graziano-Zale. I was shivering in July in my terry-cloth bathrobe. I went back to my stall, closed the metal door and threw short little punches trying to get warm.

They were back soon enough, Floyd having lost on a second-round TKO (technical knockout). His appearance—swollen nose, closed eye—did not fill me with encouragement. "Off with your trunks, Floyd. This boy has to fight soon." Floyd pulled off his white trunks with a black stripe and I put them on.

The next bout went the full four rounds. Fifteen minutes counting rest periods, the longest quarter-hour of my life. Finally an attendant looked in and signalled for the next fighter, and we started the long walk. At first I focussed on some individual faces among the sailors, guys a couple of years older than me in navy whites. Shorthaired, flattopped ensigns. One fellow with pimples around his mouth hollered encouragement to me, a southerner by the look of him. All these people who wouldn't have had anything whatsoever to do with me in normal life were cheering me on for the simple reason that my opponent was a Negro. Closer to the ring, I spotted the Negro spectators all in one section.

I glanced up to the bleachers and back again with a feeling akin to vertigo. There were too many people. The steps leading up to the ring apron were made of pine and covered with a coat of blue paint so thin you could see the grain of the wood. I got my first glimpse of Lanny Jansen when he ducked through the ropes and began to caper around the ring. Quite frankly, he looked like he could kill me. Maybe I should clinch as soon as the bell rings, I thought, and let him know I'm the wrong guy so he doesn't have to try so hard.

"Don't stand there like a statue," Guy barked. "Get loose."

I danced, threw a couple of punches, rotated my neck in circles and generally tried to comport myself like a real pro fighter ready to go to work. Then there was the ritual of the referee's instructions, during which Jansen tried to give me the bad-ass stare. I looked back blankly. The referee told us to go to our corners to await the bell. I noticed, as I turned to obey, the tiny hairs curled like pubic hairs on Jansen's chest.

There was the bell, a wall of crowd noise, the first of his punches landing. My ear felt hot and like it was swelling. My left wrist hurt on the outside from using it to block a couple of rights. I couldn't respond quickly enough to thwart his jab. I was not conscious of time. Then I was on the seat of my pants in the middle of the ring, aware of a muffled shout, with no idea of how I had gotten there. There was a flash of shock at being down, but when that passed I was seized by the horror of what had happened and how I had to get up and do something to redeem myself. I had to at least survive the round or it would be a shame I'd have to carry around for the rest of my life. I scuttled sideways and rolled up on one knee as the referee began counting. I was standing at five. He asked me if I was okay; I told him fine, sir, had just been a little off balance. Later, Guy told me I had shouted my response to the referee.

I caught a glimpse of Jansen's face as the ref waved us back together. He was wearing a cocky, superior, I'm-gonna-kick-the-shit-out-of-this-peckerwood expression. His trainer's face poked over the canvas; this guy had a process and he was laughing. I knew Jansen would come after me like gangbusters and I veered towards the ropes. Guy hollered, "Get away from there!" I didn't obey. I was doing it on purpose. Jansen came on; I clinched, spun him into the corner, and got in a couple of shots. My first of the fight, probably. He was covering up well, snaking out the jab, but I started punching at his elbows, remembering somewhere that Marciano used to do that, figuring it would have the effect, eventually, of bringing the other guy's arms down. Then I was aware of the fact that I was thinking, not panicking. I was aware of myself.

I was leaning on him, pressing against him, taking punches to my sides. Then he too began to lean, as if trying to bull me backwards. I skipped back a couple of steps, suddenly, and Jansen catapulted forward, missing with a tremendous left hook. He was off balance; I pushed out a sort of half-jab and followed with a clubbing right hand. And down he went. I waited in a neutral corner as the ref counted over him. I was two seconds away from scoring a first-round knockout; the bell rang at eight, and cornermen rushed in and dragged him back to his stool.

Back in my own corner I offered up a silent prayer that he would not come out for the second round, but it was not to be. Far from being confident, I knew damn well that fortune had smiled on me for an instant, rather than my own skills manifesting themselves. Now, I figured, the guy would be mad for revenge. When he didn't come out smoking, it occurred to me that he might really be hurt. Then I second-guessed myself, wondering if he wasn't just luring me in for the kill. He tried a few jabs but I was seeing them this time.

What happened next happened quickly, but I don't remember it in any sequence. Things seemed to shift from frantic movement to slow motion and back again. I was conscious of throwing a left hook and thinking how awkward and ridiculous it must look. I retained an awareness of punches landing, one on me and others on Jansen. Guy told me that Jansen got in one good left hand and then I just tore into him. "You just went to *town* with those right hands and that nigger went *down*!" (Throughout our brief relationship Guy would smirk knowingly whenever I used the word "Negro." "You in the south now, boy," he'd tell me. "Ain't no knee-grows this side of the Potomac, or the other side either, come to that.")

So I had won by a knockout at one minute and fourteen seconds of the second round. I felt like the luckiest young man alive.

The next morning, driving back to Petersburg with a dour Floyd slumped in the back seat, Guy said, "Boy, you learn to use your left too, you might knock some *tough* niggers down."

"No, man. I'm quitting this while I'm ahead."

I meant it, too, but I allowed him to change my mind. The second fight, a month later at the Mosque, an auditorium in Richmond, was my pro debut. The opponent was called Tom Taliaferro, and because I mistakenly assumed it to be an Italian name, I wanted to register under my given surname—Christinzio—and to say that I was fighting out of Philadelphia. Guy told me that "funny" names didn't go down well in those parts; he had needed to anglicize his own.

"Well, you could advertise it as the War of the Wops or something."

"Taliaferro is a good old southern name."

I won on the name part but Guy convinced me, rightly so, to be billed as a Petersburg boy. "You say you're from Philadelphia, you gonna have to knock this boy out to win." It was the only smart thing he told me.

This pro debut filled me with more trepidation than had the first encounter; I hadn't known what to expect before. It was necessary to look at things honestly. I was not a graduate of a Dale Carnegie course, nor had I gone to boxing school. Although I might have been of more than average muscularity, I was not in boxing condition, and had difficulty breathing at the best of times due to a deviated septum. My face would probably cut easily because it was bony and angular. My skin wasn't thick, and I had a nose that offered a particular target. Furthermore, I didn't know much. Well, I knew one thing, but knowing it didn't help. I had realized in just that one fight that a boxer's temper is his own worst enemy. It has to be subjugated. The fighter has to be in control. Me, I was generally nonchalant, and not calculating enough to initiate an attack to hurt the other person. That's why I loved sticking out the jab straight on a line from the left shoulder, not rearing back, because it didn't *seem* like a malevolent thing. But then something would happen and I'd lose my temper and get entirely single-minded about the matter. This "something" wouldn't even have to be a punch to my head; in fact, a missed punch would more likely start me off. In the instant of ducking or slipping the punch, I would have an instant to *think*, to consider the hurt that the guy wanted to put on me. The bastard.

I did have three things to offset my liabilities: speed, reflexes and the experience of scores of street fights that had been a part of growing up. These latter helped mentally rather than physically, because techniques cannot be transferred from the asphalt to the canvas. Curiously, however, there was a strange code of honour to those sidewalk encounters. Feet were never used, and even though a set-to might degenerate into debased judo-type moves it always began with fists. So I was no stranger to hitting and getting hit. I had no fear of taking punishment. But I was worried about embarrassing myself. And there was a vague, indefinable fear. The fear of the unknown, the unspeakable.

Taking all these things into consideration, I figured maybe the best thing to do was get in the Hudson and point it north. But I went to Richmond, met Tom N. Taliaferro, a white boy nicknamed TNT, and we engaged in what, to be generous, was a crowd pleaser. I knocked him down four times in four rounds and, being no Chuvalo, went down once myself. After the final bell we moved to the centre of the ring to hold hands with the referee. When the announcer said, "We have a split decision," my heart did a half gainer. To my way of thinking it was a shutout. The only round anyone could possibly have given TNT was the second when I went down—up at three—even though I came back and finished strong. I'd had him down in the first and third, and twice in the fourth. I had a horrible glimpse of going through life explaining to sceptical listeners that I'd really won the fight but had been robbed. And I would probably have to push myself to fight again to make up for it. My future was restored when the referee raised my arm in victory. That was it for me. I *knew* if I fought again I would lose. There were other things on my mind, and I knew I'd make a better beatnik than boxer.

A year and a half later I found myself broke and on the beach, Miami Beach, and needing some dough I went to the famous Fifth Street Gym to offer myself up as a sparring partner. It was an act of desperation. Hunger was doing the talking. Chris Dundee, I believe it was, shrugged, told me to go to work on the heavy bag. But after a few seconds, he clapped me on the back and said, "Kid, maybe somewhere, but not here."

Down but Not Out

Boxing has always attracted more than its share of vociferous opponents. In England, which by the mid-1800s had a two-hundred-year history of devotion to "fistiana," the location of a fight was often kept secret in an attempt to foil police, who were likely to shut down a match at the urging of local do-gooders. Boxing matches were a regular part of life in Canada's early logging and mining camps, and, by 1850, what towns there were had boxing clubs. These establishments, presided over by a "professor" of pugilism, lent a sort of legitimacy to the sport. The constabulary might endeavour to put an end to a bout held in the woods or along the shore of a lake—the theory being that the public could be corrupted by the sight—but said public was assumed to be safe from the evil influence of any fight held behind closed doors. Despite the "civilizing" aspect of the Marquis of Queensberry rules introduced in 1880—five-minute rounds, one-minute rest periods, the ten-second knock-down rule, the mandatory use of gloves—prize fighting still met with disfavour. The possibility of abolishing the sport was raised in the House of Commons in 1882, when it was brought forward by the temperance lobby, and again in 1913, when heavyweight contender Luther McCarty was killed in the ring.

The impetus for the most recent flurry of abolitionist activity on this continent came from that most reactionary of organizations, the American Medical Association. In a 1983 issue of JAMA (*Journal of the American Medical Association*), the publication's editor, Dr. George Lundberg, pleaded that boxing be banned. By early the next year, mostly as a result of a forum in *U.S.A. Today*, the call for abolition surfaced.

For the readers of "America's newspaper," Dr. Lundberg summarized his group's opposition to the sport. First, he said, "Boxing is an affront to morality because it is the only so-called sport whose principal purpose is the intentional harm of the opponent." Second, "Boxing is a throwback to bloodthirsty, uncivilized man, with spectators deriving vicarious pleasure from the violence." Oddly, not until item three was a nonmoralistic criticism advanced: "Acute brain damage is common in boxing and occasionally kills regardless of medical treatment. Every knockout is acute brain damage." It did not help the pro-boxing position to have an opposing view furnished on the same page by someone like Jose Torres, former light heavyweight champion. "There's no proof," wrote Torres, "that damage to the brain of any fighters occurred from fighting."

Boxing can cause severe trauma to the brain, of that there can be no doubt; nor can it be denied that people have suffered great injury in the boxing ring, 465 of them, between 1918 and 1988, dying as a result. Some of them were grown men over the age of twenty-one fighting for dollars, others mere children flailing away with oversized gloves in the pure amateur ranks. They came from Canada, Thailand, Korea, the U.S.A. and a dozen other countries. Four hundred and sixty-five victims; and thousands of others brutalized, it is maintained, because they watched.

Dr. Joseph Boyle, a past president of the AMA, has stated his organizations's position as follows: "It seems to us an extraordinarily incongruous thing that we have a sport in which two people are literally paid to get into a ring and try to beat one another to death, or at least beat each other into a state of senselessness that will leave them permanently brain-damaged." Rabbi W. Gunther Plaut, one of Canada's foremost boxing abolitionists, condemns the sport in a 1985 article published in *The Globe and Mail.* "The more the blood," he claims, "the greater the approval from the audience; the louder the thud with which a fighter falls to the floor, the greater the applause."

These opinions, as misguided as they may seem to those who appreciate boxing, are representative of the abolitionist position. But if the pronouncements of such critics are an accurate description of what goes on at a prize fight—two men try to kill each other or inflict brain damage while the crowd roars—does it not seem incongruous that in seventy years of boxing matches, both amateur and professional, all over the world, *only* 465 fighters have died? Indeed, it is nothing less than astonishing that a sport labelled brutal and bloodthirsty by its opponents should result in far fewer deaths than solid, middle-class sports operated, organized and sanctioned by solid, middle-class people.

Football and basketball cause more deaths by far than boxing. Dr. J. Falletta, medical director of the Canadian Amateur

Boxing Association, reported in the *Canadian Medical Journal* that 339 deaths occurred in amateur and professional boxing throughout the world between 1945 and 1982. In the period between 1958 and 1972, Dr. Falletta documented 450 deaths in high school football in the United States. None of these deaths, nor the hundreds since 1972, have provoked the American Medical Association to call for the abolition of high school football. In February 1985, when eighteen-year-old Tyrone Powell died during basketball practice at Mark Twain High School near Center, Missouri, it was the seventeenth high school basketball fatality in the U.S. that season. But there was no outcry from the AMA or from newspaper editorial writers.

When Loyola Marymount basketball star Hank Gathers suffered a heart attack and died during a game in January 1990, no connection was drawn between his death and the demands of his sport. The lead stories in consecutive issues of *Sports Illustrated* were devoted to the young man. A couple of days after Gathers's death, his team was victorious, and *Sports Illustrated* trotted out the usual cheap sentiment: "This One's for You, Hank." Gathers's death was handled like a national tragedy; had he been a boxer, it would have been a national disgrace.

By March 7 of the 1985 winter season in the U.S., there had been thirty reported ski deaths. Two of these skiers died during organized competition. That same year, Canadian freestyle skier Jim Milina learned that he had failed in his suit against the organizers of a 1981 ski demonstration near Toronto in which he was injured and became a quadriplegic as a result. Madame Justice Beverly McLachlin ruled the young skier had not proved negligence. "No duty is owed to participants in an activity such as this to guard against risks recognized and accepted as inherent in the activity," is how the Madame Justice summed it up.

The Globe and Mail has not run articles about the risks inherent in skiing. Likewise, they were silent in February 1985 when Francis Affleck of St. Lambert, Quebec, died after crashing his Ford during an auto race at Daytona Beach. They were also silent the previous September when Lynn Estrada died as a result of injuries suffered while competing at Vancouver's Exhibition Park. Estrada was the thirty-fifth jockey to die in thoroughbred racing in North America in ten years. No one called for a ban on horse racing. Similarly, there were no abolitionists heard from in 1980 after Avelino Gomez, Canada's most publicized rider, was killed. Or two years earlier when Ron Turcotte's accident sentenced him to life in a wheelchair.

There is no point in continuing the body count. There are easily a dozen sports that result in more fatalities than boxing. But for some reason boxing's detractors assiduously avoid this reality. Or, if they admit that other sports are also dangerous, critics fall back on the argument that boxing is the only sport where the opponents set out to harm each other. Colman McCarthy, writing in *The Washington Post*, declared that the object in boxing "is to injure or kill." Rabbi Plaut claims that opponents in boxing "are paid to . . . beat one another unconscious." When these assertions are measured against the undeniable proof that boxing is not as dangerous as several other sports, it becomes clear that the only solid ground for an abolitionist's opinion is one of principle, the principle of intent. The argument thus becomes a moral one, and a little digging unearths those familiar worms, hypocrisy and self-interest.

Boxing is the only major sport that can properly be deemed anti-establishment, an unspoken fact that underlies the antipathy felt towards it by middle-class people, particularly those who consider themselves slightly to the left politically. Many of boxing's critics fall into the small *l* liberal category. In the old days they were called do-gooders, and in years past they sent missionaries to put clothes on the world's aboriginal peoples. In Canada a decade and a half ago, hearts overflowing with sympathy for those "less fortunate" than themselves, they were successful in "cleaning up" the carnivals. They found it morally repugnant that deformed or unusual people were put on display for profit. The result of their moral stand was that hundreds of people with no hope of securing work elsewhere were forced from the family of the carnival and onto the unemployment and welfare rolls. The hypocrisy is no less apparent in their stand on boxing.

In the great let's-abolish-boxing rigadoon, the liberals find their dance card taken up by the AMA, which happens to be the biggest, richest and most powerful lobby group in the U.S., and which has often opposed progressive gains in the field of medicine, including federal loans and scholarships to medical students, legislation to regulate blood banks, free polio vaccination programs and free clinics for the detection of cancer and venereal disease. The AMA's biggest fight has been against any form of compulsory health insurance, and medicare was their greatest loss. The AMA has deemed boxing an affront to morality and claims the sport "exploits minority youth for the benefit of the affluent." This from an organization that refused until 1971 to bring sanctions against state and local chapters that refused to admit black doctors.

Even if you assume that boxing abolitionists are sincere and that their opinions derive from sober consideration, it is nevertheless true that the sport makes an easy target. In denouncing the "primitive" nature of boxing, critics are attesting to their own more highly evolved stature and concomitant lack of baser instincts. Boxing is barbaric, it kills and injures people; therefore, it has no place in a civilized society. Compared to more complex issues like abortion, acid rain, affordable housing and Central American puppet-dictatorships, boxing is a gift wrapped in shiny paper. The most pleased recipient of this present is the former-enthusiast-who-now-knows-better, and the best representative of this genus is American journalist Garry Wills. Writing in *The New York Review of Books*, Wills states that he gave up the sport when, at a social function in 1982, he stood near Muhammad Ali, "embarrassed by his inarticulateness, and deeply ashamed."

Wills had been one of the noisemakers on the Ali bandwagon. His sorrow is, typically, not so much for the pain suffered by Ali but for his own role as part of the mob, "urging him on, applauding the blood." Wills enjoys his wallow in guilt while having the presence of mind to align himself with the thinking of St. Augustine and the person of Augustine's friend Alypius, a boxing fan of long ago. "At the first sight of blood," wrote Augustine of Alypius, "he took a sip of animality. Not turning away but fixing his eyes on it, he drank deeper of the frenzies without realizing it and, taking complicit joy in the contest, was inebriated by his delight in blood." For St. Augustine, as for Wills, it was the crowd who suffered most, not the battlers, for Alypius "was wounded deeper in the soul than was the gladiator in his body."

Ali still functions as a symbol, making his appearance in the columns of sportswriters striving to add a little weight to their daily output. They describe Ali's introduction at heavyweight championship fights, how he makes his way across the ring with underwater steps to nod at each combatant. The old familiar chants of "Ali, Ali" quickly fade to embarrassed silence. ("Look at him, brain-damaged; he has Parkinson's disease, you know. Maybe boxing should be banned after all.") What Ali has is Parkinson's syndrome abetted, but not caused, by damage to the brain resulting from boxing. According to his personal physician, Dr. Dennis Cope, director of the Medical Ambulatory Care Center at UCLA, Ali's condition "imitates Parkinson's disease, yet does not have its degenerative pattern. From the tests that we've done, we have established that it is not punch-drunk syndrome—there's no evidence of deterioration of his ability to think. He's all there, and there's no reason to expect him to deteriorate."

Historically, sports commentators and athletes have often come from similar backgrounds. This is still true, but the backgrounds have changed. Like reporters, most athletes now are middle class and college educated. Sports journalists today do not feel uncomfortable interviewing baseball players, synchronized swimmers or downhill skiers; they recognize each other. Not so modern reporters and prize fighters. In recent decades, the gap between commentator and boxer has become wider than the distance separating one side of the tracks from the other. As other sports become esconced in the franchise fabric of contemporary society, boxing retreats farther out into extreme territory. It is not terrain for which most journalists are outfitted. A random perusal of the files of Vancouver sports sections of the thirties and forties shows three or four boxing stories daily. With the exception of a brief wire-service account of a major fight, or the notice of a boxing-related death, Vancouver papers now don't carry four boxing stories a year.

In Canada, the liberal media position on boxing is typified by Peter Gzowski, host of CBC's popular show "Morningside." Gzowski is also the author of *An Unbroken Line*, a very good book about his love for and involvement with horse racing. He makes no reference in his book, however, to the high rate of death and serious injury in racing. When Gzowski had boxer Shawn O'Sullivan on his show in 1984, he made known his negative opinions about boxing. O'Sullivan deftly feinted Gzowski's jabs and jabberings in regard to the dangerous aspects of the sport. The journalist bid farewell to the fighter by saying, "Well, Shawn, we like you, even if we're not so sure about your sport."

In an interview later that year, Gzowski talked with hockey writer Stan Fischler, who had just published a book listing the hundred best hockey players of all time. The Pecksniffian radio host was most enthusiastic when talking about hockey fights. He and his guest had the following exchange:

Gzowski: Why did you make Eddie Shore number two if he lost a fight?

Fischler: Fighting has nothing to do with it.

Why would someone want to abolish bouts between people who know what they are doing while condoning and relishing fights between people who don't know what they are doing, and in a game where "fighting has nothing to do with it?"

"Banning boxing has been tried a hundred times," wrote Red Smith, the dean of American sportswriters in the two decades following the Second World War, "but there were always men ready to fight for prizes on a barge or in a pasture or the back-room of a saloon." Some of its opponents, recognizing that this is so, propose ways to clean up the sport. Too often their suggestions are predicated on abysmal ignorance of boxing. Rabbi Plaut, for example, has suggested that "Amateurs, at least, should wear helmets and thicker gloves and only go for three rounds. The pros put on thin gloves to hurt their opponents more severely."

If Rabbi Plaut were put in charge of reforming boxing, there would be an immediate increase in the number of deaths and injuries. The gloves actually protect the hands, not the head. There were far fewer deaths in the bare-knuckle days because fighters were reluctant to risk hand injury by going for the head. And has the Rabbi ever noticed a professional fighter continually touching his forehead with a glove during a match? This is a reflexive gesture, a habit formed while repeatedly adjusting his head guard during sparring sessions. The head guard slips and slides, obscuring the fighter's vision and distracting him. The guards may be all right in amateur boxing where all punches landed, no matter where, or how authoritatively, are scored equally, but in pro fights, head guards would account for a tremendous increase in head injuries and fatalities. Would the Rabbi Plauts be around to bear the responsibility?

The best arguments for boxing's abolition are provided not by outsiders but through the machinations of those engineering the sport from within. If the sport's enemies advanced beyond moralistic mumbo jumbo and into the field of serious research, professional boxing would be in big trouble. Take the most notorious of boxing deaths in recent times, that of Deuk Koo

Kim, who succumbed shortly after his WBA lightweight championship fight with Ray "Boom Boom" Mancini in November 1982. Kim was an inferior fighter in no way qualified to be in the ring with Mancini. Yet, before the bout, he had been blessed with the WBA's number ten ranking. There is no mystery to Kim's status as a contender; it was bestowed merely as a way of justifying the match.

What didn't come out in the ensuing orgy of indignation was that Kim belonged to a peripatetic group of Korean boxers whose purpose it was to enlarge the numbers in the win columns of home boys throughout the world. During the two years prior to Kim's death, forty-seven Korean opponents shipped from their country to engage in bouts worldwide compiled a record of three wins, forty-three losses and one draw.

In 1986, boxing fans had a horrible glimpse of potential tragedy when another fighter with an unearned number ten ranking from the WBA went to the edge of the abyss. This was Canadian heavyweight Willie De Wit, whose inability to rise by ten to take more punishment from Bert Cooper may have saved him from that final count where numbers run on to infinity.

World boxing is governed by contingents of marauding alphabet boys who make run-of-the-mill managers and promoters seem like so many Andy Hardys. There is the World Boxing Council (WBC), the World Boxing Association (WBA), the International Boxing Federation (IBF) and, most recently, the World Boxing Organization (WBO). There is even a federation in Canada though it is about as significant as the fish's famous bicycle. The situation can best be described as surrealistic. Try to make sense out of the WBA, the WBC, the IBF and the WBO, and the alphabet will suddenly go Coptic or Cyrillic.

Theoretically, these organizations wield no authority over state, provincial or national federations, but in order to have a fighter ranked worldwide it is necessary to deal with them. Each controls an area of the world, or a part of a country. A

WBA champion has, for instance, to fight in a WBA area against a WBA opponent and by WBA regulations. Usually the organizations do not recognize each other's champions. They make their money from "authorization" fees paid by those promoting or holding options on title fights. As well, they take percentages from champions and challengers.

There is nothing W. C. Fieldsian to these people's larceny; they possess none of the ironic self-consciousness of the carnival huckster. Their usual territory is the venal. Their organizations cannot be adequately explained, nor their activities delineated. It is all done with smoke, mirrors and bag men.

The WBA grew out of the old mob-run National Boxing Association. Americans controlled it from 1931 until 1973, when Latins took over. The presidents come and go but the main man stays the same: one Pepe Cordero, who got into boxing after serving a couple of prison sentences for burglary. A two-part report in *Sports Illustrated* by Pat Putnam revealed the WBA's bureaucracy of deceit. After the pieces appeared, Putnam began receiving phone calls promising his sudden demise should he ever set foot in Puerto Rico.

"There's only one bag man in the WBA," Bob Arum has said, "and that's Pepe Cordero. Anytime you want something arranged in the WBA, you bribe Cordero and he takes care of it." Having promoted thirty-four WBA title fights between 1981 and 1983, Arum presumably speaks from experience.

But perhaps the best indication of the reputation of the WBA is that the World Boxing Council is considered to be more responsible.

The WBC was founded in 1963 by George Parnassus, a California promoter of Mexican and Mexican-American fighters who was unable to get them rankings from the American-dominated WBA. By the early seventies, the new group had surpassed the WBA, primarily through the efforts of Jose Sulaiman, a Mexican of Lebanese ancestry. Sulaiman, dubbed "the Mexican dictator," made a fortune by manufacturing paper used in medical tests; as well, he has extensive real estate holdings and is on the board of directors of several companies. In 1982, Sulaiman was arrested in Mexico City for allegedly trying to smuggle Mexican archaeological artifacts, valued at between $200 million and $750 million on the black market, out of the country. Arrested by the Federal District's notorious police chief Arturo Durazo, Sulaiman was held for a week and then released for "lack of evidence." Rumour has it that the bribe paid to Durazo by Sulaiman was $200,000 U.S. A year later, Durazo had to flee the country when a Mexican judge ordered his arrest on charges of bribery and running death squads.

Sulaiman got his start scrapping in the quaint and traditional "hors d'oeuvres" that precede Mexican fight cards. In the hors d'oeuvres, two youths from the crowd box each other while people bet and throw coins. Sulaiman lost all his fights but was always the winner at picking up the centavos.

Boxing historian Bert Sugar has called Sulaiman "Don King's lap dog"; writer Flash Gordon described him as "an international crime figure"; former Madison Square Garden matchmaker Teddy Brenner filed an affidavit with the United States District Court listing thirteen instances of Sulaiman's alleged extortion. Curiously enough, the one thing he has not been charged with or accused of is taking bribes. As New York State Boxing Commissioner Michael Katz put it, "It's the corruption of loyalty and friendship."

In Montreal in November 1984, at the World Boxing Council's twenty-first annual convention, Sulaiman pledged his "commitment to a renewed effort to do all that is necessary for the safety of the boxer." He announced his organization would "pioneer" injury insurance and sophisticated medical tests for fighters, including CAT scans and EEGS (presumably on medical paper purchased from El Jefe's own companies). Since other organizations already had insurance and demanded the same medical tests, this was a bogus claim, even if not so recognized by the press. The media preferred Sulaiman's announcement that WBC championship fights would only last twelve rounds rather than the fifteen of other organizations, a rule that had been in place for the past year. The shorter distance, he asserted, would save lives. History and experience, alas, do not back him up. Of the last hundred amateur and professional boxing deaths prior to the Montreal convention, ninety-eight occurred earlier than the twelfth round.

Nevertheless, Sulaiman's claims served up easy stories to reporters and created a smoke screen around his own homicidal-seeming activities. He sanctioned, for instance, the January 31, 1983, WBC junior bantamweight championship in Caracas between Pedro Romero and titleholder Rafael Orono. The challenger was ranked ninth by the WBC despite having lost his last five fights, three by kayo. Orono knocked Romero down seven times before dispatching him in the fourth round to the world of brain damage. But it was only a twelve-round fight.

With friends like Jose Sulaiman, professional boxing doesn't need to go looking for enemies. Another kind of friend boxing doesn't need is the judge in Wisconsin who in May 1990 overturned the state's refusal to grant Aaron Pryor a licence to box. Pryor, the former lightweight champion who in the early eighties was called the best fighter in the sport, plummeted to the back alleys of drug addiction, once being saved by police in Miami who discovered him naked and crying for his mother. In the spring of 1990, he was attempting a comeback. Not here, said the Wisconsin State Athletic Commissioner. But the judge, a woman, ordered the fight to proceed on the grounds that to stop it would be "infringing upon the rights of the handicapped."

Enough already. Instead of being abolished, boxing should be brought under the control of a centralized regulatory body that would appoint informed and reform-minded insiders to state and provincial commissions. Under an equitable system managers and promoters would be required to supply *verifiable* medical and performance records for their fighters. This information could be used to assemble reliable monthly ratings that could not be bought; anyone attempting to do so would be suspended from boxing for life. A centralized, workable system with enforceable and enforced strictures would not only reduce injuries and save lives but go a long way towards nullifying the attacks of boxing's critics. It might even convince them to redirect their attention to the truly dangerous sports.

Sammy and Baby

The thirties and forties were boxing's golden age, and Canada made notable contributions to the lode of talent. But none of them reflected the glitter or typified the era more than Sammy Luftspring and Norman Yakubowitz, better known as Baby Yack. Both were from Toronto's old Jewish ghetto, and both came close to winning world titles. While I was living in Toronto during the seventies I was lucky enough to meet these two fabled fighters.

Luftspring I knew from various nightclubs, particularly the Oriental Palace on Bloor Street West where he was a host always ready to turn bouncer. I didn't know he had been a fighter until someone told me. And quite a fighter he was. Luftspring was managed by Doc Kearns, who had guided Dempsey and Rocky Marciano. At the height of his career, Luftspring had signed to fight welterweight champion Henry Armstrong when he was thumbed in the eye during a tune-up bout by his opponent, Steve Belloise. He never regained sight in that eye. For someone who had boxing in his blood, it was an experience that could have ruined his entire life. Indeed, it sent him down into a personal hell for years, but eventually he overcame the tragedy and became the busiest referee in the country, as well as a popular man about town. His life has been so filled with drama and incident that it inspired a full-length motion picture.

I had been nodding hello to Luftspring for years before his autobiography *Call Me Sammy* appeared. Certainly the most entertaining book on boxing published in this country, and I said as much in a review in *Books in Canada*. The most curious thing occurred. In twenty years of reviewing books in newspapers and magazines, it has only happened two other times—the author of the book sent me a thank-you note. Sammy Luftspring and Alberto Manguel sounds, of course, like the main event at the Forum in L.A. The third author could referee, though some would question his integrity: Alger Hiss.

Norman Yakubowitz fought some of the greatest men of his era, guys like Harry Jeffra, Lou Ambers and Indian Quintana. But when his days as a fighter were over, Baby Yack did not walk so smoothly into the afterlife. Sammy Luftspring graduated to nightclubs, but Baby was a beer-parlour kind of guy. There was no movie money coming his way. On the other hand, he was not a guy it was easy to feel sorry for. There was no reason to, either.

A few people of my acquaintance had mentioned getting a cabdriver who claimed to be a great fighter in olden times. I was aware of the name Baby Yack but I didn't match him with the cabbie until one evening I was having a drink in the Silver Rail, talking to the bartender about the crowds of shoppers on the streets and the Christmas decorations in Eaton's across the way. The guy said he hated Christmas. "Yeah, the hype starts earlier and earlier every year and before too long, I know, Baby Yack will be around putting the arm on me for the retarded kids' fund. Not that I got anything against retarded kids, you understand."

"Of course not. You mean Baby Yack, the old fighter?"

"Yeah. You know, he beat Sammy Luftspring in the thirties."

"He drive a cab?"

"Sure."

I asked if he knew where Baby Yack lived.

"Who knows with a guy like that? He's a street person."

It wasn't more than a week later that I was having another drink, this time with my friend Phil Surguy, and I mentioned that I was determined to find this Baby Yack since his name kept popping up all the time. I had gone to *Toronto Life* with the idea of doing a little piece on the guy. It had been sort of a last resort, the idea of writing about Baby Yack; since he couldn't be found around the fight clubs, I didn't have any excuse to ask him questions and pry into his life. Journalism provides this opportunity. Phil had never heard of Baby Yack and didn't know anything about boxing, even if he did remind me of a handsome A. J. Liebling. But the next morning he called and said that Baby Yack would be waiting for me at noon at such-and-such hotel on Jarvis Street.

"How the hell did you locate him?"

"Well, I hailed a cab when I left you last night, and no sooner was I seated than the driver told me he used to be a prize fighter. I said, 'You're not Baby Yack, are you?' 'Yeah,' he said, 'how did you know?' "

That morning on my way to Jarvis Street I stopped in at the

Canadian Boxing Hall of Fame on Victoria Street in back of the arcade. It is run by pugilism's self-appointed publicist and oft-times ring announcer Tony Unitas, a guy who, in his carnival days, used to exhibit a seventeen-year-old albino boy as the world's oldest man. Tony allowed as how he thought the Baby wasn't up to the mark these days, having lost all his money and maybe been hitting the bottle a bit too much. I left feeling more than a little reluctant. If journalism provides an introduction to people you wouldn't meet otherwise, it also brings with it the obligation of writing about them afterwards. Maybe this was not such a good idea, I thought, if he was really down on his luck. The clichéd scenario was all too possible: "Didn't you used to be Baby Yack?" "Yeah, I coulda been a . . . you know what. Buy me a beer, will ya, kid?"

He was seated at a table in the beer parlour surrounded by a few septuagenarians in tattered overcoats. His hair was greyer than in the old photographs but it was still parted in the middle. In what weak late November sunshine managed to get through the frosted-glass windows, he looked like he was waiting not for me, but for Edward Hopper. The whole place smelled like Janitor in a Drum.

"I'm the guy, the journalist, who's been looking for you."

"A journalist? When your friend said you was from *Toronto Life*, I thought it was an insurance company."

At first he avoided talking about boxing. He mumbled something about the Jim Vipond Christmas Fund that he was involved with, and how you had to hustle just to make a decent living driving cab. For about twenty minutes, he slipped every pugilistic reference I made and countered with some homily you could crochet and frame for the kitchen wall. Then he opened up. I later realized he was just feeling me out to see whether I knew a left hook from a kick in the ass, and whether, therefore, I was worth the effort.

Baby Yack told me to call him Noomie. Referring to an old column wherein Ted Reeve had dubbed him Yack the Ripper, I said, "Come on, Noomie. You weren't one of those dirty fighters, were you?"

"Jeez. Come on, yourself. Who're you, Cinderella or somethin'? Listen, I knew how to use the thumb and the elbow and the cut glove too, I'll tell you that. But mostly the butt of the head, and I was no *dirty* fighter either. You shoulda seen what some guys done. I just believed in that old saying about do unto others. I was raised in the slum and not only that I'm a Jew, and if that wasn't enough, I'm a *little* Jew. I had to get tough early."

His folks, Barney and Bessie, came to Toronto from Russia in the early years of the century, and the Baby was born in a cottage on Palmerston Avenue. "I was born on Christmas Day and my mother was so happy about that she would have named me Jesus, if it weren't for my father advising her it was a bad idea. I mean, Christmas being a Christian thing." His parents were bootleggers, and their Baby began selling booze and newspapers on the street when he was six years old. "I was born on the street, so to speak, and I've been on the street my entire life." Baby and his family lived in the midst of the thriving ghetto of hustlers that was, as Sammy Luftspring put it, "a separate country situated right in the middle of a stuffy, strait-laced city of the dullest half-million people the time could produce."

One day when Baby was eight years old, "This big kid comes up to me, beats me up, gives me a bloody nose, steals my money. That kid, I been fighting him ever since, one way or another." The beating proved a turning point. "The day after, I went to the Newsboy's Athletic Club and started to learn how to box. I learned fast." He fought out of the Elm Grove, the Classic on Queen Street East and the YMHA under trainer Steve Rocco. Later he got a manager, Mottel Golden, and graduated to higher-class venues.

"So I start getting fights at the old Mutual Street Arena and Massey Hall and I keep winning. They gimme these trophies so I say to the promoters, 'Hey, I can't eat these here trophies you gimme.' So they smile and they start givin' me $20 a fight, which is a lot of money in those days."

The Baby began to tap his fingers one after another along the stem of the beer glass like he was playing scales on a yellow clarinet. He stopped talking in order to better remember. Then he smiled, his eyes twinkling under thick grey and white brows. "Listen, one night I'm fighting in Detroit. Still in the amateurs. I'm waiting my turn in the dressing room. Guy in an expensive suit comes in, he's only got one arm, comes in, says 'How you doin', Baby?' I says, 'Fine, just fine.' I never seen him before. After the next fight he's back, looking worried, says, 'You okay, Baby?' I says, 'Sure thing, mister.' Next fight's done and there he is looking very bad off: 'You *sure* now, you're all right?' I say 'Uh-huh.' And now it's my turn. I knock out my opponent and the same guy comes back into the dressing room smiling and lays four hundred-dollar bills in my hand. He had lost those other three fights and had bet a thousand on me to make up for it, which is why he was so innerested in my health. And I got fifty for the fight. Not bad for an amateur."

So Baby did get tough but he didn't grow up all that much. He fought as a bantamweight and, even when I met him, he was barely a lightweight, around a hundred and thirty pounds, and much of that was small, round stomach. He cradled the beer in dark little hands. His fingers were tapered and a student of such things might have said they denoted creativity and an artistic nature, at which the Baby would have laughed. Still, everyone who remembered Baby Yack remembered that he was a boxer, not a slugger, and the ring might be deemed his studio.

He was his country's leading Olympic boxing contender in 1936 but, along with Sammy Luftspring, decided to boycott the games. Harry Sniderman, who was later to own the Warwick Hotel, raised the money to send the two boys to Spain for the International Games organized in opposition to the "Nazi

Olympics." "We got to Spain just as their revolution was breaking out. We hightailed it back to Paris for a week where we met a hundred women soldiers and Marlene Dietrich. Then to London for two weeks and back home. I turned pro right away and started to make a lot of money. I got $500 for my first pro fight." He was immediately a contender. He won the Canadian bantamweight championship in his sixth fight. "This was Frankie Martin and I got $1400 for that one and $5000 for the rematch because I was the champ. Next year I beat the former world champ Indian Quintana. It was my toughest fight. But I used my head if you get my meaning. That same year is when I beat the great Spider Armstrong the two times and got $8500 each fight."

To get an idea of how much boxing has declined in popularity in this country in the fifty years since Baby Yack defended his title against Frankie Martin, you need to know there is no longer a bantamweight division in Canadian professional boxing. Consider also that the highest purse earned by Tony Pep of Vancouver in defence of his featherweight title, the next division up from bantamweight, was $5000 in 1986. He only got that much because the fight was staged by Bruce Allen, a rock promoter who had an interest in Pep's opponent, the extremely popular 1984 Olympic bronze medal winner Dale Walters.

The world championship kept eluding Baby Yack. He was the guy they didn't want to risk, the number one contender for two years. Besides Quintana, the Baby beat former champs Sixto Escobar and Harry Jeffra. "Then out of nowhere comes George Pace and he becomes champ. I got a chance at him on a rainy night near the end of 1939. We threw everything at each other and by the end of the fight we both looked like we had been through a meat grinder. The referee took us both by the wrists and led us to the centre of the ring and we was looking at each other 'cause neither of us knew who would get the decision. He got the decision."

Baby looked down into his glass and didn't say anything for a minute. His was a rough, fleshy face and although the features were small there was no delicacy to them. Yet, except for some puffiness around the eyes and ears, the hundred amateur contests, the seventy-five pro bouts and the innumerable street fights had been moderate in leaving their mark. He glanced towards the colour TV mounted in the corner that showed some idiot game-show contestants grinning outrageously. "That decision, the way that fight turned out, it still haunts me."

He assured me that he had done a lot of things in his life besides boxing, but if I wanted to look at the old fight clippings, I could come up to his room. I had been afraid he was going to suggest that. I had located an article about him that had appeared a few years earlier. The Baby was described as "a broken-down pug right out of Runyon" and his room depicted with all the relish of an overzealous supplement writer turned loose on the wild side for the first time. The guy mentioned filthy linoleum floors, cracked plaster walls, broken mirrors, dim, bare light bulbs swinging from frayed cords over a bed that sagged like a spavined horse, all in gee-whiz-isn't-it-simply-horrible hyperbole. When I entered the room, the same room, I realized immediately that the writer had possessed an imagination. If it wasn't the Windsor Arms, it was respectable: a rug, drapes, double bed, washroom, nothing more nor less than a clean room in a decent if inexpensive hotel.

Baby kept his clippings inside plastic Loblaw's bags which he took from a dresser drawer. In another opened drawer, I glimpsed sport shirts in laundry wrappers. An empty mickey of rye sat on the dresser top and eleven dead sixers of Labatt's Blue were stacked in a corner. A pair of greying underpants dried atop a silver-painted radiator. The heels of three pairs of shoes poked out from under the foot of the bed. Set apart from them and protected by a transparent plastic bag were a pair of scuffless, speckless white slip-ons. I was reminded of these particular shoes while travelling in Mexico several years later. Walking the back streets of Zihuatanejo on the eve of La Dia de las Santas, I saw through the open door of a shack a middle-aged man lying on his bed underneath a picture of the Virgin of Guadalupe. In the middle of the dirt floor were a scuffless, speckless pair of white slip-ons. When you woke in the morning, you would, if the saints had chosen to bless you, find a little reward in your shoes. I am told by the people at El Gimnasio de Boxeo in Acapulco that all Mexican fighters set out their boxing shoes on this night.

The torn and yellowed newspaper clippings conjured up the glory days, attesting that the Baby had indeed known the high life and fancy times while much of the rest of North America was riding freight trains, pinching pennies, selling apples or jumping out the windows of their brokers' offices. Booze, broads, $8500 a fight. Sixty-nine wins in seventy-five pro bouts. He was called "the heartthrob of Toronto fight fans" and "the king of the customer coaxers." He was the best and highest-paid fighter in Canada.

There was the program for the 1938 Baby Yack Testimonial Dinner, at which the head speaker described the fighter as "that dapper little fellow of the sleek hair and the sparkle in his eyes." The Baby assured me once more that he had made a lot of money. "Yeah, walked into the parlour of the old shack and handed my folks fourteen G's to buy a big house on Spadina Avenue. You know why I'm here living in this kind of place? I'll tell you why. My old man got sick after my mother died. Heartbroken is what he was. I had to sell that house to pay his hospital bills. He stayed in that hospital five years until he died."

He let his gaze circle the room. "Tommy Farr was a good friend of mine. Joe Louis used to come up and watch me fight. He used to smoke marijuana way back then. They took him for all he had. Not me. I drive a cab six days a week and I got two bank accounts. Just Monday I put $50 in the one and on Friday I'm gonna put $50 in the other. Anytime I want money I can get it from the bank. I always made money. I boxed but I did other things and made money doing them, too. Always on the street. After I quit fighting I went in the army six years and when I got out I was a very successful bookmaker. It was natural for me to do that, a street sort of thing."

The Baby had to go to work so we went down to the lobby. He pointed through the open doors of the beer parlour. "See that table in the corner? One night just a couple of months ago I'm sitting there minding my own business when this broad about forty years old comes in, a tall broad, good-lookin' broad. She says, 'Ain't you Baby Yack?' I say, 'I am and how do you know?' Turns out her mother had sent for my picture in the old days and used to have it pinned to the wall in the house. We have a few beers and she says to me, 'I want to go to bed with you; I never been to bed with a Baby.' We went up to my room. She had a bottle in her purse. You know what we did?" I told him I had a pretty good idea. He described the goings on in some detail and when he was finished, I said, "Gee, Noomie, if all that's the truth you wouldn't have any trouble going ten rounds right now."

"Yeah. Hah hah. That's pretty good. I was always popular."

He left the hotel and went to work. A couple of months after the article was published, I saw the Baby coming out of the Warwick, headed for his cab, double-parked on the street. He nodded me over and said, "Hey, tomorrow I got to see about my cab owner's licence. I may get my own cab, see. Couple of months, think I'll go down to Vegas. Guy I know there promised me a job if I want. I can deal craps, you know. I'm not gonna live in that place forever. I can change rooms tomorrow, same as I can change jobs. I'll always make out."

"Yeah, well, if you do go to Vegas, you got to remember to take those white shoes."

He laughed. "Okay, pal. See you around."

He got the car door open, then he turned back around and said, "Yeah, look, thanks, okay? Thanks for not making me out to be a bum." Then he got into the cab and drove away.

A year passed without my seeing him again, so I did some checking. The desk clerk at the hotel said he had left a few months earlier, no forwarding address. Somebody else said the Baby was living with relatives. The relatives told me they had seen neither hide nor hair of him. Another individual slipped me the information that a private investigator, hired by he wasn't saying whom, had tried to locate the Baby but to no avail. Not even certain newsboys knew anything. But a guy at the Warwick told me, "You want to see him, come around at Christmas time."

I didn't. I moved away and never saw Noomie, the Baby, again. Never heard a word about him, either, until a couple of years ago when I received the clipping in the mail. No note, no return address, Toronto postmark on the envelope. It was from the *Jewish Weekly*, an obit: "Streetfighter Baby Yack Was Boxing Champ." Above the head was the line, "Spirit and guts got him through." There was a good picture of the Baby, dressed to fight, hair combed back and slicked down, the star of David on the left leg of his trunks. I can see him that way knocking out Spider Armstrong and Harry Jeffra. I can see him too in normal clothes, having one of his best scraps against swastika-carrying louts at the Christie Pits riot. But most vividly of all I envision him double-parked on a snowy Christmas Eve in order to put the arm on a barkeep for the retarded children's fund. The guy said Noomie was out of Runyon; more out of Dickens, if you ask me.

One more thing about him. It would be appropriate if the Baby had died on Christmas Day, and he almost did. He missed by a few days. He passed away during Hanukkah.

Great White

At five-foot-seven and one hundred-seventy-five pounds, Tommy Burns from Hanover, Ontario, was not only the shortest and lightest heavyweight champion of all time, he was also the only Canadian to hold the title. To white racists of the time, Burns was also an ignominious traitor to his people, for he had relinquished the premier symbol of manhood to a black. After Jack Johnson defeated him, Burns coined a phrase and started a craze, that of the great white hope. He roamed the world looking for the white man who could smite Jack Johnson and make things right again. He never found him. In the 1940s, Burns had an epiphany, got religion and was transformed into the Ambassador of Universal Love, preaching against all forms of hatred, especially race hatred. He died in Vancouver in 1955 after one of his hellfire-and-brimstone sermons.

Some ironic symmetry could be seen twenty-five years later in the town where Little Tommy died, for Vancouver was the home of the kind of guy Burns once went looking for. Heavyweight boxing's current great white hope was Gordy Racette.

Like Burns, the young man was a former hockey and lacrosse star turned fighter. Unlike his predecessor, Gordy was a big, handsome fellow, and the fortunes of the local fight scenes were dependent on him, the only fighter west of the Rockies who could draw a big enough crowd to make a fight card a success.

For most of his career, Racette was managed by Tony Dowling, who discovered him in a So You Think You're Tough contest in 1979. Dowling had entered another heavyweight who was up against Gordy in the finals and was receiving a whipping. "How can I beat this man?" the fighter asked Dowling.

"You gotta do something dirty's the only way. Elbow him, butt him." The guy tried, but to no avail. Dowling signed up Racette. For Dowling, a manager who had been knocking for a long time, it seemed like the door had finally creaked ajar. A little bit of light came shining through, and he convinced himself it was starlight he was glimpsing.

Dowling was thirty-five years old when he discovered Racette, but that was only an official statistic. He was a lot older in experience, yet ageless in another sense. Born in Rathcool, near Dublin, Dowling ran away from home as a teenager, lied about his age and joined the RAF in Belfast. After being detailed to shake leaves off trees in preparation for a visit by the Queen, Dowling decided the air force was not for him. He enlisted in the French Foreign Legion, having been seduced, like so many others, by the romantic recruitment poster in the Marseilles train station. He was a legionnaire until learning his first assignment would be erecting kilometre signs in the Sahara. It was then he beat a less than beau-geste retreat to Algiers.

By crook and later by hook, as well as by cross, butt and an occasional jab at propriety, Dowling made his way through the world. Having learned the manly art during his collage of a past, he would blow into a town, be it in Mexico, New Zealand or Holland, and offer himself up to the local promoters and matchmakers. Among his mementos of this time are two photos taken before and after a bout in Auckland, New Zealand. Worried about what Dowling might do to his charge, a rival manager dispatched three ladies of the evening to the fighter's room the night before the match. The women brought along a bottle of brandy, and several joints just in case. In the "before" photo, a smiling Dowling is prostrate on the bed, flashing a victory sign to the photographer, the three women arranged around and alongside him. The companion picture shows Dowling propped up on the same bed the next evening after the fight: alone, nose broken, cheekbones bruised, bandage over his forehead stitches. One eye is swollen shut and Dowling stares at the camera from the other, managing just a hint of a sardonic smirk.

Dowling's boxing career stretched over two decades. His last bout was in 1980 against Jean-Pierre Coopman, who was once considered as an opponent for Muhammad Ali. The most generous thing that may be said about Dowling's performance in the match is that he was courageous enough to show up.

Dowling's drifting eventually brought him to Vancouver, where he took over a vacant and decrepit building that had housed something known as the Inner City Gym. He renovated the place, changed its name to the Shamrock, and began looking for fighters to fill the premises. He found fighters but not *the* fighter—until that So You Think You're Tough contest.

Were it not for boxing, it is difficult to imagine Dowling and Racette ever meeting, unless it was for the purpose of the former pulling a hustle on the latter. Racette was born in Prince Albert, Saskatchewan, but grew up in Port Alberni and Nanaimo on Vancouver Island, and it was the island that bounded his world until he was in his twenties. He played hockey and rugby for a couple of years in island leagues, and spent a few seasons with the Nanaimo Timbermen of the Western Lacrosse Association. Meanwhile, he worked in a steel mill and as a bouncer. He acquired a black belt in karate and took correspondence courses in weaponry and camouflage, hoping someday to become a bodyguard. With a string of barroom victories over loggers and bikers, Racette decided to give the tough guy contests a try. But he was shy, so he chose to debut away from home, in Delta, B.C. He won the heavyweight category, then repeated his success in Duncan and Campbell River before appearing in his hometown. Undefeated, he journeyed to the big event in Vancouver where he encountered Tony Dowling.

Racette had no amateur boxing experience and, except for the tough guy bouts, had never been in the ring. But because Gordy was already twenty-five years old, Dowling wasted little time on the niceties. After a couple of months of fundamentals, Dowling turned him pro. Racette won a series of fights against men who were only slightly more refined in technique than the bikers he had tangled with in the pubs. Then, in only his tenth bout, he was matched with the veteran Jimmy Young. It looked like being a horrible mismatch. It was Young, after all, who had ended the career (for a decade, anyway) of former champ George Foreman; it was Young who had beaten Ali only to be robbed of the decision. Young knocked out Racette too, but not until the tenth and final round of a hard fight. It was in losing to Young that Racette showed he just might have a future.

After that contest, Racette returned to more realistic opposition, knocking most of them out, beating them all. Then he was matched for the Canadian title against Trevor Berbick, a Jamaican-born, sometime resident of Canada more often seen in Miami. The fight was to be held in Gordy's adopted hometown of Nanaimo. The show attracted the kind of attention not seen on the west coast for fifty years. The Shamrock was discovered by the nonboxing media, people who hadn't been to that part of Hastings Street since the obligatory visit to the Only Seafood Restaurant during their University of British Columbia days.

Dowling had brought in Jimmy Young from Philadelphia and Yaqui Lopez from Stockton, California, to work with Racette. Lopez had fought for the world light heavyweight championship five times; with him were his manager Jack Cruz, who had appeared in the movie *Fat City*, and his trainer Hank Pericles, a handsome man with a deep tan and wavy snow-white hair. One afternoon Cruz and Pericles were standing by the doorway of the Shamrock viewing the ring when the scarred double doors opened and the wind blew in a man and woman, L. L. Bean–attired and toting portapaks and clipboards. The woman stopped on the threshold, glanced around and uttered a professional "Wow!" Stepping to one side and brushing past Cruz and Pericles, whom she acknowledged with an absent-minded "Pardon me," she said to her cameraman, "Get a shot from the doorway."

"Yeah," he replied. "I know what you mean; this is just like *Rocky*."

This was only the first of many times outsiders would be heard drawing a comparison to the Rocky movie. This particular reporter approached a man who was leaning on the ring apron watching Racette spar with a young middleweight named Mike Muldoon and held her tape recorder up to his face. The guy was just off the street but he was hollering things to Racette that sounded authoritative, like "Lateral movement, lateral movement!"

The reporter obviously thought he was in charge. "I'd like to ask you a couple of questions."

He looked at her blankly.

"Did you fix this place up on purpose to look like the boxing gymnasium in *Rocky*?"

"Huh?"

The fisticuffs weren't much but the staging of them was impeccable. The City of Nanaimo was the promoter of record, the pillars of the community worked their plinths off, the townsfolk cooperated by buying tickets and the weather outdid itself. There was a wonderful air to the thing—if you weren't Gordy Racette.

The mill town is reached by a ferry from the mainland. The sun came out midway through the crossing and glittered on the water as we neared the docks where little boats bobbed below the bastion; the buildings were painted in Caribbean pastels and there were even, if anyone beyond the littoral will believe this, a few palm trees on the shore. It was twenty degrees Celsius. The boat was filled with fight fans and there was palpable excitement. It was not difficult to imagine the voice of Howard Cosell guiding the boat in: "An unlikely but beauteous site for a championship fight . . . Na-nai-mo, British Columbia, Canada."

Stepping ashore you could see "GORDY" emblazoned on every business and motel marquee in tilting plastic letters. Everyone wore a smile, the barroom doors were wide open, the 25 per cent unemployment rate was forgotten, and it was like you were nineteen years old in some other era, just disembarked at a South Pacific port. It was Gordy this and Rocky that, and in such an atmosphere statistics have a way of playing tricks. The knock on Racette was his lack of experience. He'd had no amateur experience, while Berbick had been in the Olympics. Yet Gordy had engaged in twenty-four pro fights, one more than Berbick. Before Berbick gained prominence by knocking out John Tate (while Tate had his back turned), his only encounter with a name opponent had lasted the minute and a half it took for Bernardo Mercado to knock him out. Yes, the papers were saying, and the people were repeating it, anything could happen: look at *Rocky*.

Rocky Balboa was a crumb-bum smalltimer who had a hard time wearing his hat and talking to his dog Butkus at the same time. Yet he won the championship. Pure fiction, except that Rocky Balboa was based on Chuck Wepner, "the Bayonne Bleeder," who came from behind his New Jersey bar to put Muhammad Ali on the canvas, one of only four men ever to do so. Less than a year after the Ali fight, Wepner was knocked out in the tenth round in Binghamton, New York, by Canadian Horst Geisler, who in his next fight was kayoed by Trevor Berbick. Yes, anything could happen.

Prior to the press conference Frank Ney, the ever-popular mayor of Nanaimo and originator of the world-renowned bathtub race, works the room, shaking hands and looking like a 1920s racetrack tout. Also working the room is Tony Dowling, who circulates for the purpose of bragging on his fighter. The boasting is contagious enough that the usually modest and taciturn Racette tells the media, "Berbick hasn't got what it takes. He's an arm puncher. He swings wide. All I have to do is start slipping a few of those wild swings and start working on the inside, not get too carried away." When asked to reply to these comments, Berbick shrugs and smiles, "I'm pleased to be able to give the young man an opportunity."

Not even Dowling's hyperbole can match the words lavished on Gordy Racette that night in the Villa Hotel, the Tally Ho and NHL lounges and the bar at the Racquet Club. A man sidles up to a woman at the Tally Ho, puffs out his chest and says, "You know, I went to school with Gordy Racette." She surveys him coolly before replying, "That's funny, so did I, but I ain't never seen you before."

Someone else is recalling a fight Gordy had, sans Marquis of Queensberry rules, during his stint as a bouncer. "The other guy, eh? He was *totally* destroyed." Actually, it seems that the other guy had enough of himself left to provide the real inspiration for the fight with Berbick. Racette's last on-the-job tussle resulted in a court ordering him to pay his opponent $16,500 for damages.

"I know one thing," a man loudly asserts. "If they had this fight in a parking lot, Gordy'd win."

The Frank Crane Arena at Beban Park on the outskirts of town is no parking lot. The man who put the bout together, even commuting between Nanaimo and Halifax, where Berbick was then in residence, is Parks Director John Furlong, and in the wee hours on the morning of the fight he is at the arena worrying things over. The round girls, recruited from a Vancouver modelling agency, have just finished their last rehearsal. Furlong tugs at the ring posts like a guy kicking tires, sighs and switches off the lights, section by section. As we open the side doors to leave, I look back at the ring silhouetted in the moonlight.

At three in the morning a loud conversation ensues outside my hotel room window. "I got my money on Gordy," a fellow is shouting. "I'm gonna clean up."

A woman concurs. "Gordy'll kill him! He won't let us down."

I look out in time to see the woman throw her empty beer bottle into the bushes. There are two men with her; she grabs the arm of one of them and they stagger off. The other guy takes a step towards them, followed by a backward step he doesn't want to take. He has on stout work boots with the laces undone. He lurches up to a lamppost and raises his hand after his friends. "Hey!" he calls, but they are gone. The man begins tugging at the buttons on his jean jacket, then gives up. I watch him for a minute, then, just as I'm about to turn away from the window, he calls out to the world in general, "Ah, shit! Gordy, he doesn't have a chance!"

The sun shines on the day of the fight. At the weigh-in, the media besiege Racette and ignore Berbick. He looks kind of lonely standing there in his white warmup suit, so I go over. "I didn't know people were so friendly out here," Berbick says. He adds, with a wink, "Didn't know they had so much money, either." Above even the clank of the scale weights, the shouts, the scraping of chairs, the squawking chunks of tape-recorder playback can be heard the voice of Tony Dowling: "After we beat Berbick we'll go to Europe . . . the States! We got an opportunity in South Africa . . . " Off in a corner, Yaqui Lopez, one-half, with Dwight Muhammad, of 1979's Fight of the Year, is saying, "I'm going on one more year. You don't get hurt on the way up; you get hurt on your way down. Gordy, I've been working with him but I can't help him from now on. In there, you're by yourself, you and the other guy. I wish for Gordy . . . "

And if wishes were horses.

There is an intermission after the prelims, and as everyone heads back to the seats comes a swelling of music: the theme from—what else?—*Rocky*. As the lights begin to dim, Pat Benatar belts out "Hit Me with Your Best Shot." Suddenly the area is dark, and after a collective surprised murmuring, there is silence. Moments pass. The quiet explodes with the first thunderous chords of "Thus Spake Zarathustra." An arrow of light splits the darkness, finds a spot on a far wall between bleachers and expands to contain the archway of a tunnel behind the grandstand. After half a minute Racette is there bobbing in the midst of his entourage, and they begin snaking their way to the ring. The music rumbles like it is ready to be born from one of those Nanaimo coal mines; the crowd roars; the whole arena trembles.

This, the approach to the ring, is the greatest moment in

boxing. If staged properly, it hardly matters whether the bout is a local ten-rounder or the heavyweight championship of the world. It is pure drama, delicious anticipation. There is nothing to compare with it in other sports; nothing even comes close.

For five entire minutes Gordy Racette has lifted twelve thousand people right up out of their seats and out of their lives. It is his moment. His last moment.

The fight is a disaster for Gordy, who never gets unwound. He lands a blow to Berbick's head after the bell rings ending the first round. It will turn out to be Racette's best punch of the night but Berbick, who has already turned away, does not even acknowledge it. He staggers Racette with an amateurish roundhouse right in the second, beats him in the clinches in the third, muscles him to the canvas in the fourth, and so it goes until the eleventh and final round. Between rounds, Berbick, who has barely trained for this encounter, leans nonchalantly against the ropes, glancing at the ringside folk. He does not sit down throughout the entire fight. Racette, the better-conditioned athlete, slumps on his stool from the beginning, chest heaving with exhaustion, as his seconds scurry about him. He is exhausted not from the punishment he is taking but from the panic of not being able to think. You can master the entire arsenal of punches, be thoroughly versed in defensive tactics, know theoretically what to do in any given situation, but none of this knowledge will do you any good unless it can be applied under pressure. Racette spends the entire fight gasping, trying to find that small place where, simultaneous with countering Berbick's aggression—the assertion by Berbick of his personality—he, Gordy Racette, can declare himself. He never reaches the place; he backs up, he covers up, he reacts but never initiates anything. He can't; he is mentally dominated. Berbick knocks him out of the ring in the eleventh round. Ringsiders push Gordy back in but referee Claude Jutras mercifully stops the bout a few seconds later.

After the official decision is announced, Dowling puts his

arms around Racette and guides him through the ropes. As he is bending down, the fighter gives a little wave over his shoulder intended for all his fans.

Later that evening at the Malaspina Hotel, Berbick, unmarked and seemingly unconcerned about the events of two hours earlier, dines with his people, graciously accepts compliments and makes a number of phone calls. Racette, meanwhile, is in bed in his room at the Tally Ho, shivering under several blankets, clutching a bloody towel, the right side of his face nearly paralyzed. He will learn the next day that his cheek is fractured and a pin will have to be implanted to hold it together. He will pass blood for several days. But on this night, his concern is for all the people who identified with him, as if he might have assuaged the pain of the economic situation and their own bleak existences. "I let them all down," he says gallantly, pressing the towel to his swollen face. "I choked." Back in the bars, his fellow islanders show no gallantry at all, expressing exactly the same sentiments: "Gordy let us down."

Next day comes the hangover. It is as though a deal has been struck with the celestial promoter, and a defeat for Gordy means the same old island reality and the same old weather. Riding the ferryboat back to the mainland through the fogbound straits and a glowering afternoon, only Tony Dowling is given to more than groaning and muttering. "I don't believe the progress Berbick made! What being in with Tate and Holmes and Ali has done for him! We can make that kind of progress. Yes, indeed, byes. This has been a learning experience! We're going forward!"

"Tony?" I ask when no one else is around. "Are you off your rocker, or is there something else you're not telling?" He answers with a wink of the eye.

Dowling waited only long enough for the stitches to be removed before going public with grandiose predictions for Racette's future, every one of them sounding ludicrous in light of the performance against Berbick. But within a few months Racette knocked out Pete Young in five rounds in Portland, Oregon, and Big E. Smith in three in Fort Worth, Texas. He followed these with a close decision over veteran Scott Ledoux, who had been in against Kenny Norton, Mike Weaver, Larry Holmes and Muhammad Ali.

In the week that led up to the bout with Ledoux, the more experienced boxer heaped scorn on Racette. It would have been considered merely fight hype had not the Fighting Frenchman's analysis of Racette's deficiencies been fairly accurate. But to Gordy, it was just more of the "bullshit of boxing" that he detested. In private, he admitted he didn't care about glory or a world title, he just wanted to make one big score. It seemed, also, that he wanted to make his money by expending as little effort as necessary in preparation. All throughout the training period, Yaqui Lopez would despair. Here was a guy who had grown up in tin-roof, dirt-floor hovels in Mexico, who had been fighting since he was five years old, who loved the game and worked like a demon to bring out the best that was in him, who had never made the money he deserved, and who was now given the care of a gifted but lazy galoot who, whenever the training turned tough, turned on the television. Lopez, tall and lanky, is a devilishly handsome man with a battered, high-cheekboned face and slitted eyes. Shy and quiet, he would sometimes turn away from sparring sessions with a lackadaisical Racette to mutter agonized Mexican curse words.

But against Ledoux, Racette for the first time acted like a true fighter. He floored Ledoux in the first round; the surprised veteran got up and proceeded to go to war, knocking Racette off his feet in the third for an eight count. It was then that Racette might have quit the business he disliked, might have gone into his familiar shell and let defeat happen, as in the Berbick fiasco. Against Ledoux, however, he was not overwhelmed but composed; he backpedalled against the onslaught, using his mind and a heretofore nonexistent jab, and not only did he survive that third round but he fought back, eventually turning things around with a tremendous seventh round.

In the dressing room later that night, both manager and fighter engaged in prophecy. Dowling held his ubiquitous briefcase aloft as if all the secrets were inside. But as it turned out, there was no unanimity over how to proceed. Indeed, it was as if two roads headed from the dressing room. Dowling started off jauntily down one, towards that lustrous horizon, only to glance over his shoulder and see Gordy being led down the other.

What Dowling had in his case were various contracts, each offering lucrative paydays to Racette. There were three for $75,000 apiece, and another guaranteed $250,000 for one fight. Not bad money for a guy who just wanted to stay out of the mill. But there was someone else who wanted to take Gordy by the hand and show him the way, somebody to whom those figures were mere chump change. This fellow promised a life like you only see in the movies. Still, Gordy was reluctant to ditch Tony Dowling. Gordy's new wife, however, was not reluctant; she was adamant, in fact. "Gordy," she said, "you've got to do it. For God's sake, he's one of the most famous people in the world."

Yo, Gordy!

A year earlier, six months before Racette fought Berbick, *Life* magazine had carried an article about Sylvester Stallone's search for "a real-life Rocky." The piece described how the actor was interested in getting into the boxing business and wanted nothing more than to manage a great white hope. Stallone had his pal Richie Giachetti, the man who had introduced Don King to boxing and trained Earnie Shavers and Larry Holmes, scout around for him. At first Stallone was interested in a heavyweight named Lee Canalito. *People* magazine publicized their relationship but things didn't work out. It became obvious that Canalito, even if he was handled as creatively as Primo Carnera had been, would never make a champion. Then somehow Giachetti heard about Racette, checked him out and passed the word along to his boss. Stallone telephoned Gordy, made a pitch, and the fighter was ready to go. The only obstacle was that he had a contract with Dowling, and Dowling had those signed contracts with other promoters. According to Dowling, Racette told him, "Don't worry, Tony; I'll take care of you."

"In the old days," Dowling says now, "a fighter and a manager had a special relationship. The manager lived for the fighter. Nowadays, the fighter has a lawyer to watch over the manager. But the lawyer isn't there holding the heavy bag in the gym. Also, throughout history, whenever a woman came between a fighter and the manager it was all over. A fighter's woman shouldn't have anything to do with the business. Gordy not only had a wife, he had a wife who was a *lawyer*. Yeah, things began to sour."

Dowling, along with Racette and his wife, Nevis, was flown down to Los Angeles and put up at Stallone's home while they negotiated. "We were treated well," Dowling recalls. "We drank champagne. We saw a movie. Thank God, it wasn't a Rocky movie. I don't know, I guess I behaved myself. I mean, I didn't jack off in his bed."

Dowling figured Stallone was going to try and buy him off cheap. "But I brought those guarantees for other fights with me. We sat around and talked business and Stallone bullshitted about how he was beating up his sparring partners. Well, I know as much about brain surgery as he does about boxing. I had a contract between myself and Tex Cobb's people down in Houston. It offered Gordy three fights at $75,000 each, win, lose or draw. Also, I had a signed contract with Sam Blass of the Tiffany Agency in New York for Gordy to fight Gerry Cooney for $250,000. When Stallone heard that he freaked out. Said, 'I can get Gordy $20 million for a Cooney fight!' 'Twenty million,' I said, 'yeah, and when was the last miracle?' It was the man's ego talking, and his ego is as big as the great outdoors. But Nevis believed it and wanted to sign and I was going to get a percentage of everything that happened."

The trio flew back to Canada and no sooner was Gordy in the door than he got a call from Stallone. "Forget about the Irishman, Gordy. Get rid of him." Racette agreed that it was time for a parting of the ways. Dowling threw Stallone's $20 million talk back in the actor's face, saying, "I figure if you're going to get him $20 million for one fight, then as the man who made him and holds his contract, I should be worth a measly 5 per cent of that. So I'll settle for a cool million." Dowling settled for $40,000. "What I knew and what they didn't see at all was that Gordy, God love him, couldn't fight. Didn't want to fight. Stallone bought a dead horse."

There was a going-away party for Racette at Nanaimo's Racquet Club. Giachetti was there with his scarred and pockmarked face, wearing brass-tipped cowboy boots and a cream sports jacket over a V-neck cashmere sweater with gold chains in the V. He smoked long green cigars. "I hate the guy," Dowling told me. "His *mother* hates him." Later, Giachetti looked around at all the smiling faces and shook his head as rock music played. "I can't believe this, a going-away party for a boxer. Back in Cleveland when I went away for a fight, I was lucky to get a handshake at the Greyhound station."

The best fight of Racette's career was an eighth-round TKO over former Holmes sparring partner Leroy Diggs. It was Gordy's debut with Tiger Eye, Stallone's boxing operation. I happened to watch this fight, broadcast on ESPN, in a pub in Sidney, British Columbia. I remember the bout distinctly because I had to make the last ferry to the mainland, and if it had gone the distance I'd have been stuck on the island. As I leaped up from my chair and headed for the car, I heard pub patrons expressing their optimism about Gordy's future by loudly chanting the current champion's name: "Holmes! Holmes!" What we had observed was a good-looking white heavyweight beating a classy-looking black fighter. For all the world, Racette looked like he had it made, was on his way right to the top. But events that shaped his future transpired beyond the ring.

In L.A., things went wrong for Racette from the beginning. Stallone had promised him his own apartment, but when he arrived at the designated address it turned out to be Canalito's, and Lee was still there. No sooner was the former protégé gone than Giachetti's son moved in with Gordy. Stallone had offered Racette a Jaguar as a signing bonus, and he got one, only it was from a leasing company. "Plus it was the wrong colour," Racette grumbled. One evening while the fighter was asleep, Giachetti's son took the Jag out for a spin and the next afternoon Racette discovered it had a bent frame. When Racette offered to give him a fat lip, the kid telephoned his old man in Cleveland.

"Stallone kept making these big promises that he never kept. He didn't even keep the little ones," Racette claims. "Like after Diggs I went to Fort Lauderdale and knocked out Tom Prater. Sly had promised me a suit if I won. I never got it. I had a sore neck. He promised he'd get Franco Columbo, the bodybuilder who's a chiropractor, to work on it but he never did. I couldn't even get new boxing shoes from him."

By September 1983, when I went down to Las Vegas for Gordy's fight with Tony Tubbs, Gordy and Giachetti weren't even speaking to each other. Racette had pleaded with Stallone to get him another trainer, and the actor had hired Ray Notaro, owner of the Left Hook Boxing Club in La Canoga, California. Notaro had trained Stallone for *Rocky III*, replacing his usual man Jimmy Nickerson. "Sly didn't like it," Notaro said, "when Nickerson went around saying that Robert De Niro was the toughest of the boxing-movie actors." Racette got along fine with Notaro, a grey-haired, unassuming man who smiled a lot.

On a Wednesday afternoon, in one of the Emperor's Rooms

at Caesar's, Racette was having his last workout prior to Friday's bout. Notaro was all praise, watching with pride as his charge pounded the heavy bag. Giachetti slipped into the room and seated himself on a table in the back.

"I've only had Gordy two weeks," Ray said. "But he's coming along. He was awkward but we're ironing that out. This kid is championship material, believe me. But I do wish I'd had a little more time to prepare for the fight. We didn't know it was on until ten days ago. Still, he'll beat the guy. Gordy is too powerful for him. He's in great shape too, don't worry."

Notaro glanced quickly over his shoulder, indicating Giachetti. "These people were ignoring him. But Gordy's doing good now. I got him running three miles a day, backwards."

"Backwards?"

"Yeah, makes him agile. I'm gonna make a boxer out of him."

I nodded but inside I groaned: a *boxer* he was never gonna be.

When Gordy was finished on the bag, he climbed into the ring and lay down on the canvas. It didn't seem an appropriate place for a fighter to be, even when doing sit-ups with his trainer holding his ankles.

I walked back to Giachetti, who said, "Tell 'em I'm gonna bring a big fight up to Vancouver in a coupla months." The second thing he said was, "Whatta you been talking about with him?" Then he said, "Gordy looked real bad his last fight."

In those three sentences, Giachetti illustrated why Racette didn't get along with him: jive, paranoia and tactlessness. But it's the jive, backed by bucks, that keeps the sport going, and in the world of pugilism, a paranoid is a guy with facts. As for tactlessness, it should be the least of the things a fighter worries about. Boxing is not a finishing school.

After dinner that evening I went with Gordy on a boxer's night out in Vegas. We walked the strip, cut through the casinos, had a light beer and called it quits before midnight.

During our little tour, two things became apparent. The first was the depth of Racette's bitterness towards Tiger Eye; the other, the fact that the guy is a sex symbol.

When I had mentioned earlier to Notaro that we were going out, he said, "Oh, oh. Hanging out with the guy in public is amazing. The way the girls check him out. First time, I couldn't believe it. Know what Gordy says to me? 'Don't worry, Ray. You'll get used to it.' " Young or middle-aged, single or married with husbands in tow, the women unabashedly gave him the eye, the come-hither look and even the occasional discreet darting tongue. In one place the manager had to tell our waitress to pay some attention to her other customers. All the time I was thinking how much he could make in endorsements if he was heavyweight champion of the world. I was also thinking that the whole experience was no boost for my own ego. "Yeah, I know how you feel," Gordy sympathized. "It's like in Fort Lauderdale when I went out with Stallone after the fight. The women walked over me to get to him."

But most of the conversation concerned his problems with Tiger Eye and with Giachetti personally. Giachetti had told me, "You know, Gordy, he ain't too bright." Now Gordy said, "Giachetti, he's so awful, he hired a hooker a couple of nights ago and even she refused to sleep with him."

As we were saying goodnight, we saw a guy strapped into a wheelchair out front of the Imperial Palace. He had neither arms nor legs, and a sign hung around his neck: "I don't want your sympathy."

"Jesus, how can he live?" Racette wondered out loud. "A guy like that. No matter what your problems, they're nothing."

Gordy's problems may have been nothing much in the scheme of things, but they were all he had. If he already felt neglected there was no surer reinforcement than the door of the construction trailer parked in a warehouse in back of Caesar's, where he was supposed to change and hang out until his fight.

There were several of these trailers adjacent to the tennis courts. On the door of each, a sign painter had lettered the names of the occupying fighters. But on the trailer Racette was using, the only names were Carl Williams and Bert Lee. Below them was a piece of yellow note paper held in place by Scotch tape, on which someone had scrawled in ball-point, "Gordon Racette." He had been instructed to be in the trailer at 4:00 P.M. but he didn't fight until after the main event. There were about ten matches on the card, so this meant a wait of at least five hours. He lay on his back on one of the tables and kept repeating how he wished there was a television. He remained stolid and miserable. I had to go and watch the other fights to keep from getting depressed.

After Bobby Czyz beat Bert Lee, the luminaries began to drift in for the main event, the rematch between Aaron Pryor and Alexis Arguello. Gene Hackman, David Brenner, Carl Weathers and Jesse Jackson. Bruce Allen, the rock manager and promoter from Vancouver, John Matusek, the football player, and Tex Cobb, whose fifteen-round beating by Larry Holmes occasioned the retirement of Howard Cosell from professional boxing. Cobb was telling stories at ringside but interrupted one to grab my shoulder with a meaty paw and inquire whether I wasn't a pal of Gordy's. "Tell him to come to my party after the fight."

In the next match on the card, Carl "the Truth" Williams, sometimes called "the Heat," used his left jab to tear apart one Percell Davis. Davis had been beaten in his last fight by Al Newman, who had once been knocked out in the first round by Tony Dowling.

A game but outclassed Alexis Arguello lasted four rounds with the devastating Aaron Pryor. Half the audience left after their fight, and Racette and Tubbs had to push through a departing mob to reach the ring. The paths of the two fighters met; Tubbs gave Racette the shoulder and bulled past him. Racette's expression was glum.

Earlier I had asked Mr. Tubbs, who was carrying an extra fifteen or so pounds around his middle, if he knew anything about his opponent. "Don't need to know nothing," he glowered.

"You see him work?"

"I seen him work out with the Heat. He's gonna remember Las Vegas as the place where he fell."

It took ten rounds for Racette to fall. Tubbs just pounded away, round after round of unanswered blows. It was even worse than with Berbick, almost as if Racette were taking the beating to prove to everybody that his dislike of boxing was justified. Some maniac in the stands shrieked over and over, "Who's your mother, Racette? Boy George?"

After sitting stunned through the first five rounds, I realized the outcome was inevitable. I drifted towards Racette's corner like a pedestrian to the scene of a car crash. Gene Hackman was standing by the ring post while Gordy gasped for air between rounds. "This is terrible," he said. "Terrible. They should stop it!" Notaro peered through the ropes and shouted to us, "He's got a bad cut in his mouth. He's breathing blood."

Racette had auditioned for Great White Hope and decided, as if for spite, to play Masochist. The absurdity peaked when, at the beginning of the tenth round, Tubbs knocked Gordy through the ropes. Notaro threw in the towel, hollering for the referee to stop the bout. But the referee neither saw the towel nor heard Notaro. Some sadist at ringside snatched the blood-stained white towel and hid it behind his back as Racette groped his way back into the ring to take more punishment. Miraculously, he lasted out the round, and then, mercifully, the show was over. The last I saw of him, Racette was climbing into the ambulance to go and get stitches in his lip. He never made Tex Cobb's party.

I had the good sense not to call Gordy on Saturday. On Sunday he said he wanted watermelon for his sore mouth. "Tomorrow, I'm getting in my car and driving to Vancouver. I'm through with these people; I've had enough of this shit."

Stallone fired Notaro the next day. In parting, Notaro called Giachetti "a disgrace to our Italian heritage," and Giachetti told him he would punch him in the mouth except that Notaro was wearing a Tiger Eye T-shirt and "I'm loyal to my employer."

When I got back to Vancouver, I took a deep breath and phoned Stallone, who said, "I got nothing to say about it. I'm going away and making a movie with Dolly Parton." Tiger Eye put out an announcement that Racette had gone back to Canada to "relax." In reality, they were done with him.

A year later, Racette sued Tiger Eye and got to keep the leased Jaguar. He never fought again, at least not as a pugilist. He returned to the martial arts and won something billed as the North American Kick Boxing Championship. He became part-owner of a tavern that failed.

"I saw Gordy just last week," Tony Dowling is saying at the end of 1988. "First time in over a year. He came by the house, came through the door just as big as life. I said, 'Gordy! What in hell are you doing?' He said, 'I'm looking for a job.' When I first met him ten years ago, that's what he told me he was doing, looking for a job.

"Oh, well. We had some good times and some bad times, Gordy 'n' me. It was a heartbreak but—you know something? I'd go through it all again."

Body and Soul

Look in any boxing magazine, this month's or one from fifty years ago, and you will see a picture of Jamey Ollenberger. On this particular day in a delicatessen in Vancouver's Gastown, two tiny gold boxing gloves dangle from a chain hooked through his pierced left ear, but otherwise it is the same face that was reproduced back in '38 above a caption that read, "Crowd-pleasing Counterpuncher." Your father, your grandfather and your great-great-uncle saw a guy like Jamey Ollenberger go to war in the smoky clubs of bygone days. He is the sharp Chicago ringmaster in the Nelson Algren novels, the guy digging an uppercut to the stomach in a George Bellows painting. He is the boxer, the real goods, the guy you never heard of.

He is twenty-nine years old now, walking with a cane, and has just sent "fifty dollars' worth of clothes" to his little daughter in Winnipeg for her birthday. "I wish I could see her," he says. But her mother took off with the kid and he just split up with a cocktail waitress named Angel. Wherever we are over the course of several days—the delicatessen, a bar, a health club, walking down the street, sitting on a park bench—people greet Jamey, many of them women who seem thrilled to see him. Some make comments that might be developed later should he care to do so. "I don't know," he says blushing. "Women have always kind of liked me. Maybe it's my nose." Ollenberger has escaped ninety-six amateur and twenty-six professional fights with a cowl of scar tissue about his eyes, and with his nose thickened just enough to make him self-conscious.

In the last years of the eighties, his luck has been nothing but bad. Boxing politics kept him inactive for thirteen months, then he took a fight in London, England, on short notice, only to have the bout stopped prematurely and given to his opponent. Nevertheless, he showed so well that he signed for a lucrative engagement in Brazil. Then, back in Vancouver, he was thrown from his motorcycle by a car that swerved into his path. His right leg was shattered. "My foot was turned all the way around. Before I passed out, I reached down and twisted it back. The doctor said if I hadn't done that, I would have lost my foot." But the injury has meant the end of his career, and boxing has been the focus of his life since he was eleven years old. It is in his blood.

Ollenberger was raised in the False Creek area of Vancouver. "When I was eleven years old I saw the first Ali-Frazier fight on television, and I knew what I wanted to do with myself. My mom didn't want me to box; my dad thought it would be good for me. I joined a boxing club. There were a lot of good fighters in Vancouver in those days. At least thirty top guys, like Gordy Lawson and Steve Toehill. There were clubs and regular shows and you could fight once a month."

Ollenberger eventually fought out of the Kingsway Boxing Club where he was trained by Michael Olajide, Sr. "I'll say one thing for Senior despite what happened later, he inspired me. Yeah, he was a good inspirator—if that's a word."

Jamey had an extremely successful amateur career, winning the Golden Gloves seven times. The Golden Gloves were started in 1929 by the *Daily News* in New York City, and have been held every year since, organized by regional amateur associations. "Kids in the neighbourhood used to ask me why I was in boxing and I had to tell them something so I said I wanted to make the 1980 Olympic team. They used to kid me but then there I was B.C. Golden Gloves and Canadian champion and I was on the team. But, of course, that was the boycotted Olympics. I went to the alternate Olympics and lost the gold medal to Donald Curry [the future world welterweight champion]. I enjoyed boxing more than team sports because you depend on yourself. I got satisfaction from it because it was individual and rugged. You could take your frustrations out on the bag so you didn't have to take them out elsewhere, like on the streets, though I never went around looking for trouble."

As an amateur Ollenberger travelled to Africa, Finland and Greece, as well as throughout Canada and the United States. "The travelling was one of the best things about my career in boxing, amateur and pro. These places, you hear about them in school, but you have no idea of them really until you experience them. Boxing allowed me to expand my world. Most people have to save up all year for a two-week holiday and where do they go? Hawaii? And all the time they're worrying about how much everything costs. When I went somewhere, it was business *and* pleasure. I could relax. I wasn't paying for it. I went around the cities, saw things and met people and learned. Then came fight night and it was my business.

"In Greece we fought right out where the gladiators used to fight the lions. You changed where the gladiators and lions used to stay before they went out onto the field. During our fights sixty thousand people were there every night, outdoors on those ancient stone seats of the arena. It got you high just being in that atmosphere."

Michael Olajide, Sr., began having trouble with the amateur boxing associations, as he would later have trouble with just about everyone he encountered in the professional boxing world. "So because of these disputes, he decided to turn us pro, his son Michael Junior and me. Mike made a lot of promises. We were to get a thousand for our first fight, fifteen hundred for the second, then two thousand. It was exciting to think we'd make that much money. But all that got totally diminished. I earned three hundred for that first fight in Victoria, beating Perry Evans, and, of course, Mike took his cut out of that. He never showed me a contract for any fight, and I had to take his word on the purses. At that time the fighter didn't see the contract for a fight.

"My dream was to build myself up with a series of fights, then win the Canadian title and get a world ranking. But most of Mike's promises never came through. When Junior got to be my weight it was like I was around just to be his sparring partner. Then once, in Victoria, the promoter said to me, 'Your opponent won't fight you, he's going to fight Junior instead.' Three times it happened that my opponent became Junior's and I didn't get to fight. I got so discouraged, I quit for eleven months."

Mike Senior has been heard to say that Tony Dowling stole his fighters, Jamey being the prime example. "Tony never stole me," Ollenberger insists. "I wasn't fighting and I ran into Tony and he said he could get me fights. I knew he could because he was the big thing around Vancouver then. That's when he had Gordy Racette. Tony was honest with me. I would rather have quit for good than have gone through more promises that didn't happen. Tony never lied to me."

Dowling made good on his promise to get fights for Ollenberger, and wherever these bouts occurred—Vancouver, New Westminster, suburban Cloverdale, and later in the States and England—Jamey gave the crowd its money's worth. He was the kind of guy every smart promoter wants on his card in order to be guaranteed at least one successful bout. Whatever it took, Ollenberger was ready to do it, rumble or stick and move. You couldn't put him in over his head because he rose to any occasion. And because he was basically a counterpuncher, Jamey made inferior fighters look better than they actually were. Boxing fans, like jazz buffs, are not necessarily schooled in what they are witnessing. So although the crowd may have liked Jamey Ollenberger, they never favoured him as much as Dale Walters, for instance, a fighter of vastly subordinate abilities. "Yeah, I never stood out in the limelight. I had enough to beat fighters but I was not a star in many people's eyes."

It was just this perception of him that kept Ollenberger from getting the proper backing and the sponsorship that would have led to a world championship fight. But he was always prepared for that light to shine. He learned his business and kept in shape. When I first knew him, Ollenberger was holding down three jobs: grounds keeper and gravedigger at a cemetery during the day, aerobics teacher at night, and a Saturday stint moving furniture at a department store. Somehow he managed to put in his hours at the gym, and to fight.

"Sure, to some people that might make me sound like a fanatic but I figured the more I knew and the better shape I was in, the less chance I had of getting hurt. You don't get hurt from a lot of fighting but from not fighting enough. From not being prepared. You need 150 pro rounds before you really even reach the level of a journeyman. After 150 rounds, a guy's been in with punchers, slick boxers, maybe even a couple of bums, and you learn from them all. Probably the worst guy I faced was Jesse Toro. He was a one-armed fighter, all he could throw was the left hook. He was a little guy, 147 pounds but only five-four, and he was in his thirties when I fought him. Oh, I beat him up badly. He was there for me to hit, a punching bag. He was tough though. I stopped him in three rounds, and I learned from the fight. A guy like that can get you frustrated.

"I like to fight punchers. On the other hand I have trouble with boxers. They give me a hard time because I'm a boxer myself. My first ten fights, I warred with opponents because everybody told me I had to knock out people. I tried to prove I was a puncher. But then I realized I didn't have to do it for anybody else, just for me."

After his tenth fight, he signed with Dowling, who began sending Ollenberger to Stockton, California, to train with Yaqui Lopez and Jack Cruz. "I was the only white guy there except for two trainers. There were twenty-five fighters, blacks and Mexicans, four or five trainers, and ten or fifteen blacks and Mexicans standing around watching. I swear the whole gym stopped when I walked in and everybody turned to look at me. I worked two days without sparring, then when they had a chance to see what I had, everything was all right, everybody was friendly.

"Jack Cruz introduced me to his fighters, there were seventeen-, eighteen-year-old fighters who'd had maybe seven pro fights and they knew tricks I'd never even heard of. A trick happens to you once; a thinking fighter doesn't let it happen again. Like, if you're dropping your left and always getting caught with a right hand, that means you got to get the left up or move to the right so you're not going to get hit by that right hand.

"You learn the tricks, how to make fighters throw the punch you want them to throw, how to set them up. You drop the left because you want him to throw a straight right so you can get your hook in there. Now, when he drops his left, I'm going to feint him to see what his first reaction is, and I'll know whether he's waiting for me to come forward and throw a punch, or else I'll feint twice and he'll react after that. The feint is one of the most important things in boxing, because you make a fighter either come to you or go back, and he loses his train of thought. Unless you're a big puncher always trying to dominate a fighter, it's like a chess match. It's a thinking game. But, of course, you have to have the basics too. The hand speed and timing. You need to be relaxed and confident. The amateur fights helped me in that regard when I turned pro. Having fought in Africa and Greece and Europe, having that experience.

"The experience certainly paid off when I fought Gate Gonzalez. It was my biggest thrill in boxing, it gave me my best sense of self-satisfaction even though I lost. He was number two in the WBC, number four in the WBA. He had kayoed everybody in the top ten but they wouldn't give him a title shot. Too tough. They sent me down to be a respectable opponent, and I wound up being the only guy ever to go the distance with him. I thought I beat him and most everybody else did too. But he got the decision. Afterwards, he said, 'You're great, man, you're great.' "

Ollenberger proved to be more than just an opponent for Gate Gonzalez, but that is generally the role of Canadian boxers venturing onto the U.S. boxing scene. South of the border it is reasoned that a Canadian's record, of, for instance, 10 and 2, has been established on inferior Canadian talent. The fighter might not be as accomplished as an American whose statistics are, say, 10 and 7, but the numbers look better.

Fighters in Canada simply do not get the opportunities and exposure available to U.S. boxers. Ollenberger believes that for professional boxing to flourish in Canada, it has to be fed from a healthy amateur program. But most amateurs don't want to make the jump from three-round fights to four-, six-, eight-

and ten-round professional contests. And a kid cannot win a pro fight with the pitty-pat punches that often suffice in the amateurs; he will suddenly have to contend with real punchers. In amateur scoring, a one-punch knockdown counts for less than three inoffensive jabs.

The belief that the pros need to be fed by the amateurs presupposes the very existence of professional prize fighting in Canada. Reports of its demise may be exaggerated, but not by much. Given the paucity of cards, a kid from the amateurs would have to be a bit of a masochist to make the jump.

Ironically, it is often the case that the better a Canadian fighter is, the worse his chances are. On April 21, 1990, Ken Lakusta and Tony Morrison had their rematch for the Canadian heavyweight championship in Red Deer, Alberta. The Canadian Boxing Federation rankings appeared a couple of days earlier. The heavyweight division consisted of the champion, Morrison, and only three contenders. The light heavyweight category showed just a little better, with a champ and four contenders. The only full division, with ten contenders, was the middleweight. This meant not the best so much as it did the only. As Toronto promoter Vince Bagnato once said, "Go out on the street, find a guy between 147 and 165, sign him up and you got a middleweight contender."

Lakusta took a split decision from Morrison in a truly uninspiring battle. Having fought each other twice, Lakusta and Morrison have, barring a freak occurrence or the seasoning of Olympic champ Lennox Lewis, exhausted their money-making possibilities in Canada. But both can fight regularly in the States as opponents. In professional boxing there are categories of individuals whose purpose is to be served up as victims to more skilled fighters. There are tomato cans, bums and opponents.

A tomato can is a guy who is going to lose. He does not have to be told to lose; it is just inevitable because he is not equipped to do anything else. A bum is only slightly better. There are actually sheets circulated among managers that tout these individuals. Whatever their records may appear to be when published in the local press, no pretense is made on these dossiers. Guys with records like 1 and 13, and 0 and 11. I remember seeing the sheet on Lakusta's opponent for a match in Vancouver in 1983; the guy had lost twenty-three times in twenty-four outings.

Opponents occupy a more lofty status. The presumption is that they will give a decent account of themselves before succumbing. Even among opponents there are gradations. Lakusta is more highly regarded than Morrison since it is likely he will last longer before being knocked out, mainly because he is a tougher brawler. Morrison's main claim to fame is not his brief possession of the Canadian heavyweight championship, but his first-round knockout of former world heavyweight champion Leon Spinks. In 1986, Morrison was kayoed in one by the young Mike Tyson; the next year, he was stopped in five by Willie Edwards, a light heavyweight.

Among opponents there exists today one true legend, a throwback, a veteran of over two hundred professional contests, Bruce "the Mouse" Strauss, who is right now probably in his car roaming North America looking for work. The Mouse compares himself to Jesse James. "I go into some local hero's town, shoot it up, get blasted in the end by the good guy. Then I go somewhere else and do it all over again. I love it."

There's another category just above opponents: journeymen, guys with good skills who are always in condition and who will give a good account of themselves, maybe even win. In the twilight of his career, Ollenberger was slipping from contender to journeyman. Even so, he was slated as Hector Camacho's comeback opponent in October 1988 only until Camacho's advisers saw him work. They brought in another Canadian instead, Rick Souce, who was stopped in four rounds.

The boxing clubs in Canada, whether above a garage on Lansdowne Avenue in Toronto, below the Astoria pub in Vancouver or down an alley in Halifax, are littered with broken dreams. What do you do if you're Tony Pep, a six-foot, one-inch featherweight with all the talent in the world and no place to display it? If you were American, Mexican or a citizen of any of a dozen other countries, you might possibly be a world champion. But, as it is, you are a Canadian with no one to test you, no one to bring out all that latent talent.

What do you do if you're Jamey Ollenberger?

He was the first Canadian to appear in the cable network ESPN's popular boxing tournament to establish North American champions. "When I qualified for the tournament I went to Nike, Adidas, to local businesses, looking for some kind of sponsorship or just something like a *robe* that would say "Canada" on it. I was proud to be representing my country. But nobody was interested. Then my bosses at the graveyard said I had to choose between boxing and the job. They wouldn't give me a leave of absence to train for the first fight. So I quit that job. Before the first fight, Tony Dowling told me this was it, my big chance with plenty of exposure." He won the bout. "Thirty million people had seen me fight but in Canada I still couldn't get any backing. People offered me jobs, but I had two of them already. What I needed was to buy time to train. Then [Vancouver stock promoter] Murray Pezim got ten stockholder friends to put in a hundred dollars each to help."

Back down to Las Vegas he went, and in a sensational fight on July 26, 1986, beat highly favoured Ali Kareem Muhammad. I watched the match at a Mexican restaurant flanked by a mission drop-in centre and a pub catering to boosters and low-rent junkies on a street midway between the cheap stores of Hastings and the tourist haunts of Gastown. The restaurant had been taken over by boxing fans that afternoon, mostly friends of Jamey's, and you could feel the excitement build as fight time approached. It was a fine, friendly group, and a representative of the antiboxing legation would have been disconcerted by the contrast between the scene inside the restaurant and that on the street.

Jamey came out of his corner like a champion, and throughout the bout displayed every technique, trick and bit of natural ability he had learned or been blessed with. The crowd cheered every punch that landed. Jamey's common-law wife of the time sat with her head averted from the screen, talking to, or at, a female companion who was watching the fight. Whenever Jamey did something special, someone invariably said to her, "How about that!" or "You see that?" and her reply was invariably, "I can't watch, I just can't watch."

During the last round, Ollenberger's girl friend did something very strange. Jamey had won just about every round, and had the fight wrapped up; he came out to put a little ribbon and some decoration on the package, was slipping punches and letting fly with picture-book combinations. With less than thirty seconds remaining in the fight, and the crowd going wild, his girl friend leaned across the table and shouted to me, "Have you ever read Gogol?"

I glanced at her briefly. "*What?*"

"Gogol, you know, *Dead Souls* and all the rest?"

"Sure, sure," I replied, turning my attention back to where it belonged.

The bell. Close-up on Jamey, who raised his left arm knowing he had won the fight. Tony Dowling was making his signature gesture of twirling the towel like a lasso above his head. The decision of the judges was announced: Jamey by unanimous decision. His girl friend said, "Well, it figures."

"Yeah," I replied, "it was nearly a shutout."

"No, no. I mean, I figured you had read Gogol."

If his close loss to Gonzalez had been his greatest personal achievement, the victory over Muhammad was the peak of Ollenberger's public career. But in Canada enthusiasm for his skill and his future did not extend much beyond that Mexican restaurant. He returned to Vancouver and the big letdown. The local papers carried a brief wire-service item about Jamey's victory, but there was nothing in either *The Globe and Mail*, the "national" newspaper, or *Maclean's*, the "national" magazine. Around this time, however, a Toronto paper ran an entire column-length story concerning a cold that Shawn O'Sullivan thought he had caught in the gym. But O'Sullivan was, after all, the Olympic silver medallist from the Big Smoke, possessed of what the daily scribes decided were "choirboy looks." Ollenberger was a tough-looking boy from 3000 miles away.

"There was nothing happening for me here, no sponsorships," Jamey said later. "I was to fight Ramon Santana for ESPN's junior welterweight title and a brand new Buick in, supposedly, five weeks. I wanted to stay sharp but then the fight was postponed. In the meantime I was offered the chance to fight Alexis Arguello for $25,000. I wanted it but we were told if I took that fight I'd be out of the ESPN tournament. And after the tournament, win or lose, I'd been promised I'd get a bout with Gene Hatcher, the number one contender. So we stayed in. The fight was postponed another time and, with no job, all I did was train. I overtrained. I ran eight to ten miles a day, six of them in the sand. I rode my ten-speed five miles back and forth to the gym. I sparred four-minute rounds, and carried my trainer Bill Kennedy around the ring between the rounds. I went ten rounds on the heavy bag, six on the other bags. And I was wearing leg weights sixteen hours a day. I knew in my heart it was wrong . . ."

Just *how* wrong was evident from the opening bell in the showdown with Santana. Ollenberger might have narrowly taken the first round, but he was not the same fighter who had been in against Muhammad. It was like another young man came in his place, an imposter who looked like Jamey and was mimicking his moves. Nevertheless, it was a close fight until the last couple of rounds. Ironically, a different Ramon Santana was also in Vegas that afternoon. Known for his aggressiveness, Santana hung back, perhaps mystified by Ollenberger's left-handed style. But Jamey's punches had little authority; they were arm punches. By the seventh round, he was exhausted, backing up, operating purely on heart and reflex. He lasted the distance and didn't get hurt but he lost the fight, and didn't drive home in the Buick. "In boxing, if you lose, you're in the dressing room by yourself, that's truly the way it is."

After that final ESPN fight, it seemed like Ollenberger's whole world was recast. It wasn't only that one bad thing happened and was followed by another. And another. No, the change was in the air all around him, like he walked in a grey cartoon cloud of misfortune. There was no explaining it, either. The sweet things turned sour. His girl friend left with the baby and no warning. He took his despondency to the gym, tried to pound it into the heavy bag and sweat it out in calisthenics. But it was only in the ring that he could be himself, and fight after fight was postponed.

Then a bizarre thing happened. Jamey was the semi-main event on a card staged by Bruce Allen at the PNE Agrodome in February 1987. His opponent was Mario Rodriguez, a boxer with a record of 20-6 who had come up from Yakima twice in the previous two years and beat local boxers George Sponagle and Johnny Herbert. But with Ollenberger, the slick and powerful Rodriguez was in tougher. While the decision was by no means lopsided, Ollenberger was clearly the unanimous winner. After the official announcement, Ollenberger turned in the ring, arms upraised in victory, but he appeared stunned. The crowd was booing him. Jamey, the crowd pleaser.

He had come to the end of the line in Canada. No junior welterweight category is recognized by the Canadian Boxing Federation, and he was not going to get a chance at the welterweight title. His only hope of a decent purse was against Shawn O'Sullivan, and there was absolutely no way the handlers of the fair-haired Cabbagetown boy were going to take the risk.

Manager Tony Dowling dispatched Ollenberger to Los Angeles, where he was to be under the care of Alex Freed. "Alex assured me I would be taken care of. I could devote myself to training and not have to worry about hustling a living.

When I met him down there he took me to dinner and gave the waitress a hundred-dollar tip. Later, as I was going on my way, he gave me twenty dollars for my food for the whole next week. The apartment I was supposed to have turned into one crummy room. But in the gym I trained under Eddie Futch, who liked me. Mel Greb tried to get me fights but something would always happen. I don't know what but I know he didn't like Tony Dowling. Months went by, and then I signed to fight Angel Pedroza in Las Vegas. Two hours before the fight, a Nevada official came into the dressing room with a doctor, and the doctor said I had failed the neurological test, and the fight was off. The doctor who said I had failed, I had never even seen the guy before."

Not long after this disaster in Las Vegas, Jamey gave me the same neurological test when I ran into him on the street. He took my hand and held it in his. Then, using the key to his apartment, he scratched something on the tip of my index finger. "What was that?" he asked.

"Hell should I know?"

"We'll try it again. I'm going to draw a number from one to fifteen, and you tell me what it is."

"Three."

"No, it was eight. Try again."

"Six."

"No, nine."

I was zero for two. Jamey explained that he had missed two out of fifteen on this most sophisticated of tests. The test had been administered three weeks before his scheduled fight, although he was not informed that he had failed until he was in the dressing room on fight night.

"See, the real story," said Jamey, "was that my opponent's manager suddenly got the opportunity for a more lucrative fight. But to take it, they had to get out of this one. A deal must have been made with someone in the Nevada Boxing Commission."

But the licencing imbroglio was only beginning. The B.C. commission, Franz Kafka evidently presiding, revoked Jamey's licence on the basis of his having failed the American test, although a neurological test is not required in British Columbia. Don King had promised Jamey a fight on the undercard of the Tyson-Spinks spectacle, June 27, 1988, in Atlantic City. But Ollenberger couldn't fight without a licence. Phone calls and letters passed back and forth. When the issue was not quickly resolved, King dropped Jamey from the card. It was only when Ollenberger threatened to sue that he got his licence—too late for Atlantic City.

At the last moment, Dowling found him a place on the card for Barry McGuigan's comeback in London, England, also at the end of June 1988. Ollenberger went overseas with Tony Pep, who had work as McGuigan's sparring partner. Jamey had only a couple of weeks to prepare and he hadn't fought since his ill-received victory over Rodriguez fourteen months earlier. His opponent was George Collins, whose record was 30-0 with twenty-seven knockouts. "That record was built on local fighters. Before the bout started the referee told me there was no standing eight count. He said it to me a couple of times between rounds, which I thought was strange. I said, 'I won't need it, I've never been stopped.' "

Before the fight, Collins's people, evidently realizing they had gotten more of an opponent than they had bargained for, had the bout changed from ten rounds to six. "Even rusty and out of shape, I think I was beating him and would have gotten the decision but then in the last round, he hit me four times, I got him back twice and the referee stepped in and stopped it with only twenty-three seconds left. 'You've taken enough punishment, mate!' 'What punishment?' I said. But that was it."

That was the fight, and the boxing career, because a few days later, after returning home, Ollenberger was involved in the accident that almost cost him part of his leg.

Now, several months later, Ollenberger has a part-time job, and teaches boxing two nights a week at a college in New Westminster. "I'd like to build a stable of amateur fighters. Later maybe move into the pros with them. I have good contacts and a good reputation in boxing. People know I'm honest."

Jamey Ollenberger will never be the guy mumbling in the back of a cab about what he could have been. He may never have been the glitter of boxing, but what he has been is the body and soul.

Golden Boy

The first time I ever saw Donny Lalonde was at a press conference in Vancouver during Grey Cup week, 1982. Some masters of bad timing had chosen the day before the big game to host, of all things, a fight card. Sports fans, in a football frenzy, were not about to divert their attention and their dollars to pugilism, even if the main event was the light heavyweight championship of the world, between that nice guy but uninspiring fighter Michael Spinks and his Peruvian challenger Oscar Rivadeynera.

Or, maybe, *especially* if it was a light heavyweight championship. These poor guys, weighing no more than 175 pounds, comprise the most unpopular of divisions. They lack the dramatic power of the heavyweights and the speed and agility of men in the smaller classes. If the light heavyweight category were a literary genre, it would be the novella.

So if the light heavyweight champion of the world garnered little respect, imagine the status of Don Lalonde, he of the yellow hair.

"Who's the big mouth?" a guy asked me.

"Supposed to be the light heavyweight champion of Canada."

The man's grunt indicated what that was worth.

The reason the fellow called Lalonde a big mouth was because the fighter was reciting a poem about his own splendid abilities and what he had in store not for his own opponent on tomorrow night's fight card, but for the world's champ, Spinks himself. As Lalonde bent to the next stanza, the television lights found brown roots.

Spinks listened to the rhyming prophesy with an indulgent smile. He had gone from a St. Louis housing project to an Olympic gold medal, then back to the projects and a job in a chemical plant warehouse. He shortly quit the job and turned pro, saying he figured that "boxing was a lot safer than chemicals."

On fight night, Lalonde was introduced as "the Robert Redford of Canadian boxing." From my seat way up in the bleachers of the PNE Agrodome, I couldn't see if he blushed. Lalonde had won his title four months earlier on a tenth-round knockout of the mediocre Roddy McDonald. I had seen McDonald fight on a few occasions in Toronto. The last time was at the Ted Reeve Arena. That card was memorable to me not because of McDonald and his Cape Breton tartan trunks but for the reaction of my female companion to the proceedings. It was a first date; she was a dancer and bodybuilder with an interest in physical culture of the kind that displayed the individual body in stylized movement. But she had never been curious about boxing.

One of the preliminary bouts offered a black kid from Detroit against a local white boy. The sweat glistened on the highly defined muscles of the Detroit fighter. He gave his best bad stare to the local kid, who appeared to be there as the result of a cosmic mistake. His skin was fish-belly white and he had no muscle tone whatsoever. His brand-new boxing trunks seemed like a bad investment. The black kid, with processed hair, was wearing swim trunks. He was a picture of the hunger and determination of the ghetto. "This is terrible," said my companion. "The white kid doesn't have a chance."

"Well, wait and see," I said. The disparity in appearance was so great, so downright ridiculous, in fact, that I was seized by the notion that the white kid *had* to lay a beating on the black kid. The incongruity of the situation required it. After the three-round thrashing was over—having been stopped by the referee as blood poured down the American's face—my date exclaimed, "Hey, boxing's interesting. Nothing's really the way it seems."

But my intuition was not working on fight night at the Agrodome on November 25, 1982, when Donny Lalonde faced his opponent Akbar Muhammad from Philadelphia. Here was another guy with the ghetto in his step and on his countenance, so filled with pride that he had divested himself of the slave owner's name. There was no way this young man from my old stamping ground was going to lose to a blue-eyed, bottle-blond devil.

Lalonde answered the bell moving like a puppet manipulated by a spastic master. He kept his left hand down around his waist, slipping rather than blocking punches, and it seemed like he was trying to cop a black style but couldn't quite get the steps right. Suddenly, in the third round, Lalonde caught Akbar Muhammad with a devastating right and that was it. Who in hell is this guy? I wondered.

"He's a bum," said Tony Dowling when I inquired. "You see him, he does everything wrong."

"Yeah, but he still won."

The second part of Dowling's statement was correct. Lalonde had poor lateral movement and a tendency, when in trouble, to square off, planting his right foot even with his left. Nevertheless, the raw talent was there, and I couldn't help but wonder what would happen if he took his act down to the States. How would black audiences respond to that low left hand and the blond hair?

No one knew much about Lalonde. He certainly didn't look like a fighter. He didn't look like Robert Redford either, more like a guy who had done time as a teenager for some high-spirited crime like auto theft for the purpose of joy riding, and was now determined to lecture other youths in hopes of keeping them out of the big house. Later I would meet his manager Jay Coleman, who, while admitting he knew nothing about boxing, passed around colour glossies of Lalonde. In one, Donny was attired in a white dinner jacket and red boxing gloves. The other featured the fighter wearing plenty of pancake make-up, evidently to hide traces of adolescent acne. The photos came in a folder that hailed him as the Golden Boy, a reference, Coleman told me, to the gilded figure atop the provincial building in their hometown of Winnipeg.

According to Coleman, Lalonde was a high-school dropout, and he invested his fight winnings in old homes that he fixed up to sell at a profit. He introduced me to the fighter, who said, "Thanks," in a soft voice. I answered, "You're welcome," but wondered, for what?

Another kid on the card that night had attracted some noise around Vancouver, not so much by his own actions as by those of his father. Michael Olajide, Sr., had been touting Michael

Olajide, Jr., as the hot new thing, future middleweight champion, first of Canada, then the world. Junior had turned pro in Victoria on October 30, 1981. He was excitable in the ring. He got knocked down twice by his opponent, Stacy McSwain of North Carolina, but went on to earn a split decision.

But it was Lalonde who impressed me, and I began to follow his career. Or tried to follow his career. There is a paucity of boxing reportage in Canada; the fan of women's junior amateur lacrosse is better served. And with few exceptions, those who do write about prize fighting in Canada have scant idea of what they are doing. But not even boxing people could supply more than opinions about Lalonde, and most of these were not flattering. Hell, none of them was flattering. Lalonde was a bum. Lalonde got his victories over well-chosen stiffs. Lalonde was not a real fighter, more a dilettante who'd get his comeuppance if he ever summoned the courage to get in tough. Vague rumours circulated that Don Lalonde was a "kook," whatever that meant.

The fighter soon acquired a new manager, or at least someone to assist him in lining up fights. This was a childhood pal named Bill Ballenger, who kept me supplied with clippings as Lalonde piled up victories: defending his Canadian belt against Jimmy Gradson, knocking him down three times and out, in the first round of their Winnipeg fight; travelling to Indiana to dispose of Carlos Tite in two; defeating Don Hirtle in six in Winnipeg . . .

By the time I saw him fight again, Lalonde had won a string of matches against mediocre opponents, invested his money wisely with the help of his old friend Ballenger, been stopped by Willie Edwards, gotten David Wolf as a manager, secured a top ten ranking and won the crown from an aging Eddie Davis. Nearly five years after first encountering the Robert Redford of Canadian boxing, I was on a plane out of Toronto bound for Port-of-Spain, Trinidad, where Lalonde, now the light heavyweight champion of the entire WBC portion of the world, was to defend his title against former WBA champ and local hero Leslie Stewart.

Every so often I had approached Canadian magazines with the idea of doing a piece about Lalonde, but they were not interested in boxing unless the subject was a De Wit or an O'Sullivan. This didn't change even when Lalonde began to speak out against child abuse, confessing that he himself had suffered the beatings of his stepfather. The fighter also admitted that he was a vegetarian.

But Donny Lalonde made a good boxing story for another reason: he was nothing less than the great white hope of the moment. Sure, the heavyweight champion of the world may still be the ultimate symbol of manly attainment, but white heavyweights evince no grace or beauty. They plod, they lumber and they lurch, all the while absorbing punishment. Better for the Caucasian element to turn pale attention on a lighterweight division than to suffer continued affiliation with such a sorry lot of stumblebums. And since men in many other sports are bigger than heavyweight fighters, anyway, it hardly mattered that Lalonde was a light heavyweight. Better to have a blond-haired, blue-eyed, intelligent, thoughtful and well-spoken one-hundred-and-seventy-five-pound young man represent your race than a hulking, two-hundred-and-twenty-five-pound, "duh, ya know whad I mean?" kind of guy.

As we taxied to a stop at the terminal gate in Port-of-Spain, everyone stood up, and I immediately spotted somebody who had to be a boxing guy. He had sallow skin, curly grey hair and glasses. He took a square case from the overhead luggage bin. In that particular yet indefinable way, he *looked* like a boxing man.

He was Ralph Citro.

"I'm working the corner for La-lon-day," he told me.

Citro is one of the few individuals in boxing about whom you never hear a bad word. He is a one-man clearing-house of boxing statistics, producing a computerized record book every year out of his home in South Jersey. Citro had also been Tommy Hearns's cut man for a decade and had worked La-londay's fights for the past few years, tending between rounds to any facial swelling, cuts or contusions, and trying to prevent these from occurring in the first place.

As we stepped down onto the tarmac, I heard somebody calling, "Ralphie, Ralphie, wait up!"

It was Pete Goldfield, boxing photographer and New Jersey neighbour of Citro's. Although I was meeting them for the first time, I felt like I'd grown up with these guys. At least, I'd grown up with their younger counterparts.

Customs was typical, nonresort Caribbean. Dirty floors, faded posters, three scarred wooden booths with stamp-wielding officials. The lines were made up mostly of nationals, but there were also some disappointed-looking tourists bound for connecting flights. You could read their thoughts: "Ugh! I hope Tobago isn't like this."

One guy stood out among this latter group. He was an old man in a pale yellow leisure suit, cowboy boots and cowboy hat. A long unlighted cigar protruded from his mouth. On the other side of the customs barrier some dark-skinned guys called to him, "Mar-tee!" This was Marty Cohen, a boxing legend. More than a representative from another era, he is a representative from the era before *that* one. He had run the famous St. Nick's Arena back in the thirties. He looked seventy-five but was ninety-two. As vice-president of the World Boxing Council, he was the organization's official in charge of this bout.

There were two cars for the boxing group. We were dispatched to the "world-famous upside-down hotel," the Trinidad Hilton, where the elevator takes you down to your room and up to the lobby. That was about all this overpriced and rudely staffed joint had going for it, except that it was fight headquarters. Being ensconced in the Hilton was like being washed up on an island of boxing. And the survivors of the shipwreck were as variegated a crew as ever inhabited an exotic isle. They ranged from the fabulously wealthy to tap-city grifters who'd somehow scored a free plane ticket. The entire social spectrum was represented, high class to no class, "from the guttermost to the uttermost," as Don King would say. If there is any truth to the belief that character can be discerned from the study of an individual's face, then half this gang should have been arrested.

Marty Cohen could usually be found holding court in the lobby or the restaurant. He was like the don to whom others came paying respects or seeking advice. But he was also a reflective *capo de capos* spinning yarns that expounded upon, and depended upon, the naiveté of boxing people. Whether worn on the sleeve or hidden under a silk suit and behind a smirk, this ingenuousness is usually somewhere to be found, along with the ingeniousness that is the other side of the boxing coin.

The attention paid to Cohen was not in deference to his age. He seemed to have total recall of dates and facts. His stories didn't ramble; although they often took a few side trips, you could count on some gems being discovered on these detours. He might start out on Broadway, hop over to Coney Island and swing down to Miami, but he'd be back to pick you up outside the stage door and walk with you over to the old Madison Square Garden. "Runyon used all of us in his stories. He was an unhappy man, was Damon. And there was Heywood Broun, Ring Lardner and Winchell, but the best of them was Dan Parker of the old *Daily Mirror* and other papers. He was straight as they come, tall and straight in posture and a straight arrow; absolutely incorruptible. I remember him warning me when Jim Norris first came on the scene as commissioner."

One of those most attentive to Cohen was Bobby Cassidy, assistant trainer to Lalonde and himself a number one light heavyweight contender in the late sixties. Cassidy was tall and curly-haired, just beginning to get a little thick around the middle. This bout had some poignancy for him because he never got the title shot he deserved during his own career. It was not a matter he brought up but when asked, wrinkled his nose and shrugged, "Ah, I could have gotten in the ring with either of these guys."

Cassidy was eating dinner and Cohen was at the table with an unlighted cigar in his mouth, one of the choice Havanas someone smuggles to him in Florida. "Hey, Marty. How many of those you smoke in a day?"

"I guess about seven."

"Yuck. How long you been smoking them?"

"Since I was a kid. I stopped once a few years ago. Stopped for six months."

"Didn't it improve your health?"

"No, my doctor told me to start smoking them again. See, I had a colostomy. I had cancer of the colon. I have to travel around now with this bag. Know what I mean? I got to do my business in a little plastic bag. Uh, is this ruining your dinner, Bobby?"

"No, no, it's all right," Cassidy muttered through a mouthful of ribs and rice.

"So I get cured of the cancer but it scared me so much I thought I better give up my cigars. Doctor told me I seemed dispirited. But he figured it was a natural reaction to the operation and adjusting to the bag. But then later, he says, 'Marty, how come I never see you with a cigar any more?' I told him I quit and he says, 'Did smoking them make you happy?' 'Yeah,' I answer, so he says, 'Well, start smoking them again.' And I did and I been fine ever since."

The whole crowd was in Trinidad. The main-event referee was Marty Denkin. I knew him from *Rocky IV*, in which he had played the referee for the big showdown in Moscow. This chore had led to other cinematic imitations of his real-life trade. In fact, Denkin carried eight-by-ten glossies with him everywhere. One afternoon we were seated by the pool with two friends of Leslie Stewart's manager, one a construction millionaire from upstate New York, the other a New Orleans doctor. Also present were two women the manager had provided as companions for his friends. The women were not impressed by the fact that Denkin had worked dozens of championship boxing matches, but his role in *Rocky IV* conferred legitimate star status upon him and they eagerly accepted autographed pictures.

The morning after I arrived there was a press conference in the hotel banquet room. Stewart was sullen and broad-shouldered. In profile his head resembled an Easter Island statue. He looked about twenty pounds heavier than Lalonde, whose suit jacket had padded shoulders.

Five years earlier, at that press conference in Vancouver, Lalonde had been a kid trying to gain a little attention. Now he was a man in control. Stewart took the microphone first and succinctly declared his intention to win the WBC crown. He was about to sit down when his manager muttered something to him. Jimmy Cavo is a tall, thin Italian in his late thirties who wears dark suits with white shoes. For the majority of humanity with whom he comes into contact, he has a look of disdain. Whatever Cavo said to Stewart encouraged the fighter to add a nasty footnote to what had been a gentlemanly speech. In this bit of unpleasantness, he questioned the integrity of both Lalonde and his manager David Wolf. When it was the champion's turn, Lalonde allowed as how this was not the first time the Stewart camp had denigrated his party. Furthermore, he assured his listeners that he would take these statements into consideration while conducting business on Sunday afternoon. He spent the rest of his speech talking about child abuse.

"This is a matter that means a great deal to me. Being the champion gives me a platform to speak out against child abuse which is a big problem all over the world. There is no way I am going to lose my championship and the platform it provides. Thank you very much." The blond boxer was then besieged by female reporters, whose paeans would appear on the morrow.

Later that afternoon I went with Pete Goldfield to the stadium to watch the final workouts. The driver was a sixty-year-old East Indian man who volunteered the opinion that Lalonde was going to win the fight handily. I thought he was just being ingratiating until I saw him back at the hotel taking bets from some of the black guys who lounged around the parking lot. He had his reason: "Leslie got married recently, you see. A bad move before a fight."

Inside the stadium and under the grandstand, a ring was squeezed into a corner against a backdrop of crumbling cement. The heavy bag and the speed bag were in the corner diagonally opposite. The floors had not been swept since Raleigh won his first match with King James and took the island back from the Spanish. (It was James I speaking of Raleigh rather than Louis about Conn who uttered the immortal line, "He can run but he can't hide.") There were half a dozen black guys hanging around and when I appeared—a white fellow near their age and with no identifying reason for being there, like Pete had with his camera—they began to signify, though not ostentatiously. It was a test of sorts. Rather than stick to the corners and the conversation of the usual white folk, I went over and found a seat as near to the middle of the group as I could. This was a surprise, and after preliminary banter the jive tapered into boxing talk.

By the time Stewart arrived for his workout, Gil Clancy was there with an entourage of yuppies from CBS. Clancy, former manager of Emile Griffith and George Foreman and successor to Teddy Brenner as matchmaker at Madison Square Garden, was doing the colour commentary for the network.

Stewart was accompanied by his trainer, a rubber-faced man named Wildred "Bear" Bartholomew. Five of the half-dozen black guys cheered Stewart and turned on the sixth because he did not. This worthy defended himself by going on the offensive, declaring vociferously that Lalonde was going to win and win big. There was a large, benign-looking man watching

Stewart work out, and as the contender dug hooks into the heavy bag this fellow's shoulders rolled almost imperceptibly. I was told he had been Caribbean heavyweight champ in the late forties. He was known as Gentle Dan.

As Stewart worked up a sweat, his white T-shirt stuck to his chest and you could see the cut of his pectoral muscles. He had big upper arms and thick forearms. The trapezius muscles were bunched atop his shoulders. He had everybody "ooohhhing" and "aahhhing" as he pounded the bag. I knew he was going to lose. It was in his eyes.

He was trying to keep up a front, not coming on belligerently but showing he was in control. His eyes were doing their best to smolder but the fire was not going to catch.

There is no science to this, of course. You can't always tell. But this time I could. It wasn't the look that Michael Spinks wore a month and a half later when he went into the ring against Tyson—no attitude there, just eyes that said, "Get me the fuck *out* of here." No, Stewart had the same look in his eyes as Alexis Arguello did when I saw him come striding from his trailer at the back of Caesar's to go to meet Aaron Pryor in their rematch of 1982.

My feeling of certainty was not challenged even when Lalonde followed Stewart into the workout area looking for all the world like a participant in some gentler athletic endeavour—racquetball, perhaps. Physically, he was in no way intimidating. He is lithe with no fat whatsoever, but neither does he display any impressive muscular development. Certain nonboxing individuals have been known to entertain the notion that, hell, they could beat up Donny Lalonde. After a couple of drinks, they're sure of it. Easy to overlook is that right hand whacking the bag. Lalonde proceeded to the speed bag and the group shifted with him. But I held back looking at the heavy bag. The last shot left a dent that was very slow in filling out.

After the speed work, Lalonde lay down on the mats. His brother Darren stood astride him, bent down, placed his hands underneath Donny's spine and pulled upwards. Gil Clancy took this in, snorted and turned away with a smirk. An exercise like that, and all Lalonde's talk about meditating and being a vegetarian: it was all just a bit too new age for a guy like Clancy. He considered Lalonde an affront to boxing tradition and to Clancy's own accumulated wisdom. The broadcaster was privately predicting Stewart by an early knockout. Ironically, I had just finished reading Teddy Brenner's excellent little book *Only the Ring Was Square*, in which the former matchmaker for the garden advances the opinion that Clancy, who in earlier days was always pestering Brenner for spots for his fighters, is himself not a real boxing guy.

Back in May 1985 in Winnipeg, Lalonde had fought Willie Edwards, a former world contender. Lalonde was then without a manager and he promoted the fight himself. He floored Edwards early in the bout but didn't have the ring savvy to finish him off. Edwards knocked Lalonde out in the ninth and burst the Golden Boy's bubble. But Lalonde remained positive. "I proved," Lalonde said shortly thereafter, "that I knew enough to fail big." He also knew that if he wanted to continue and be a success in boxing he would have to get some astute guidance. He went looking for managers in the States but was repeatedly rejected because of his unorthodoxy. Then he found David Wolf, who had developed his boxing contacts back in the sixties while sports editor at *Life*. As a manager Wolf had two notable successes, two champions: featherweight Luis "Sharpshooter" Espinoza and lightweight Ray "Boom Boom" Mancini. There had also been a great white hope that didn't happen, Duane Bobick, and one outright disaster, former football player Ed "Too Tall" Jones. What Wolf could do best was move a fighter. He moved Mancini, who had heart but limited abilities, to his championship, negotiating a $2 million contract for him to challenge Bobby Chacon. At the time, it was the largest purse ever earned by a lightweight.

Wolf realized two things about Lalonde up front—that he

was extremely marketable and that, although he had potential, fighting was not natural to him. To bring out that potential, Lalonde would have to be handled with care. Wolf turned him over to Teddy Atlas for training. Atlas was a young guy near Lalonde's age, and Wolf figured they would get along. They didn't. Atlas was young in years, but old-fashioned in outlook. His regimen didn't work with Lalonde. "Atlas ran things like a military camp," Donny said. "I'm more of a free spirit."

"Lalonde's a flake," Atlas responded. "And a fake."

Atlas was succeeded by a former New York Golden Gloves winner named Tommy Gallagher who, although from the old school himself, accepted Lalonde the way he was. "I told him, 'The hell with what you can't do, we'll work on what you can do and get you doing it better than anyone else.' " One afternoon in the hotel lobby, Gallagher offered a concise summation of the difference in their characters. "Donny's a man of the eighties," he shrugged. "Me, I'm a man of the fifties." Actually, with his high-rise slacks, flat-brim fedora and Irish, sidewalks-of-New-York demeanour, Gallagher more closely resembles a man of the forties, a Dead End Kid grown up.

The next morning I took a walk from the hotel into the centre of Port-of-Spain. Near the Hilton complex, old men sat on benches in the scraggly shade of dry, forlorn-looking trees and stared at the empty race grounds. Black and East Indian school kids ran by. I cut into a narrow street, thinking it would be cooler. Walking along a prison wall, I heard the shouts of men in the big yard. Across the way three prostitutes loitered by the door of a restaurant near a chalkboard that advertised, "Lunch Special, $6 T.T."

About a block further on, without warning, it started to rain, and suddenly the streets emptied. I saw an antique shop and went inside. The front of the shop was crammed with porcelain figurines, pictures and boxes of prints, but towards the back were tables heaped with used shirts and trousers. Sitting on a small stepladder was a fat black girl in a caftan. The owner was a tiny white woman, maybe fifty years old, smartly dressed in skirt and blouse and medium heels. She told me she had come to Trinidad from France in the early sixties with her husband, an engineer. He died ten years later but she stayed on. She liked the country, or she had liked it until the oil boom ruined everything. "People who never knew money suddenly had money. It changed them. Then the oil boom collapsed and the bad crime began. They are now back where they have been but having had a taste of what money can buy. It is very bad here. I would like to move to Martinique."

I found a small, framed painting of a scene from the walls of Pompeii. It was signed by an Italian artist, and dated from the last century. I bought it for five Trinidad and Tobago dollars, about three Canadian. The French woman showed me some plaster statues of saints. I narrowed my choice down to two.

"Why are you in Port-of-Spain?" she asked.

"For the boxing match."

"And who do you think will win?"

"Well, I have to go with my countryman."

The girl in the back rocked on her stepladder seat, smiled broadly and patted her thigh. The shop owner pointed to the taller of the two saints. "Since you are here for the boxing then you must choose this one." I looked him over. He appeared as pious as the other one but the plaster hand that protruded from his faded robes held an arrow.

"St. Sebastian," said the French lady. "The patron of athletes."

The rain had stopped and the sun seemed to pulse as it dried the streets. A woman gave me directions, walked a couple of blocks with me and talked about Saturday night's annual battle of the calypso bands. It was to be held at the national football field, the same site as Sunday afternoon's contest. The main drag was jelly-tight, hawkers cheek by jowl along the shop walls shouting imprecations and pleas—some in rhyme—to buy shoelaces, batteries, wind-up cars and chewing gum from them alone. Most of the hawkers and loiterers were black, the shoppers East Indian.

I went into the only restaurant I could find, a plasticized chicken shack. There was a sign over the door with a yellow chicken's head on it. The bird looked like a degenerate. The tables had deep cigarette burns and the cracks in the chairs were covered with Day-Glo tape. The food was slow in coming and not worth the wait. It was nearly noon, and the disc jockey on the radio signed off for the weekend with these thoughts: "Dere are few tings certain on God's green earth / But I tell you, mon, dis I know for sure / By tomorrow afternoon they will be a new light heavyweight champion."

As I was crossing the central park with its hard-packed earth and white-painted border stones, three teenaged black girls waved for me to stop. One of them stepped forward, hands folded at her waist; she seemed about to say something but faltered. Her pals nudged her with their elbows and she blurted out, "Are you here for the prize fight?"

"Yes, I am."

"From Canada or United States?"

"Canada."

"Oh, do you know Donny personally?"

"Well, as a matter of fact, I do."

She fairly beamed, rose up on tiptoes and kissed me on the cheek. "He is such a nice-looking man, Donny is."

Then the other two came forward ceremoniously to kiss me. Over their shoulders I happened to notice some curious onlookers. The girls ran away giggling. The noon whistle blew and the streets cleared faster than they had when it started to rain.

Back at the hotel, Dracula was skulking around the dining room. Chalk-white complexion, red lips, big dark eyes, black hair in a widow's peak, suit more appropriate to a blustery afternoon in Bucharest, Don Majesky wanted someone to talk to, someone to make a deal with. He was itching to plan future fight cards in locales ho-hum or exotic. Drac had to make something happen.

Phone him at home in Queens and the message tells you he has gone to Australia. The switchboard operator at the Regency on the Rocks says he just checked out to catch the first leg of a flight to Paris. What the man does cannot be summed up by a handy designation, no matter how vague; he is, for instance, more than is contained in the popular obscurantist label "consultant." He is sort of like the ultimate utility man in baseball, a guy who can catch an inning, pitch an inning, snare one on the warning track, make you a deal on a gross of bats or option you to Syracuse. But baseball people, no matter how utilitarian, don't do their work under the grandstand.

Majesky brings people together and coaxes a result, or else gets fed up and does it himself. He advises, he makes matches, he promotes, while others take the credit. He has an encyclopedic knowledge of the fighters, trainers, managers, promoters and commissioners of every country. If you need ten-ounce gloves in Savu Savu, Don's the man to call.

"Gordy Racette would have made some good money if he hadn't of got mixed up with Stallone . . . Ollenberger's a wonderful kid . . . Olajide could still be a good fighter if he gets away from his old man; I'd like to see him fight Hilton. I'd take Hilton . . ."

Outside on the pool deck I ran into the doctor from New Orleans. He was holding a glass of green liquid with an umbrella on top. A short round man, he was wearing shorts and an open terry-cloth beach shirt. His legs were thick and hairy. His bald head was peeling. He told me that back home he had a sideline working for a small hospital that provided health care for the elderly; he admitted it was an ongoing problem to do the job adequately and still make a profit. Every time I saw him he wanted to discuss the physiological aspects of the punch to the head. "I don't see how a guy can withstand the effects of a hard blow to the temple."

"Well, you're the doctor, but it seems like the most devastating blow is the one to the chin."

"I don't see how that can be worse than one to the temple."

"Evidently a punch flush on the chin knocks the brain back against the top of the skull. The shock is greater because the brain has a longer way to go than if it was jolted sideways. At least, that's the way I understand it."

"Hmm, could be, you know. I'll have to consult my books. By the way, which one of those guys is Lalonde?"

He pointed to four beefy rugby players who were on holiday from Wales. The smallest one was about six-two, 220 pounds. They were partying and rugbying their way through the Caribbean.

"None of them; Lalonde's over there." I motioned to the other side of the pool, where Donny was stretched out on a plastic lounger talking with his girl friend and his brother.

"That guy? Come on, you got to be kidding. He looks like the young lawyer in the movies who gets the girl. He doesn't have a chance against Leslie."

The next day, the doctor backed up his opinion by laying down a yard with the East Indian cab driver, who was now driving us to the stadium—the doc and me, the construction guy who was Cavo's mentor, and Don Majesky. As we neared the stadium, our pants sticking to the leatherette seats, Majesky whispered to me that he didn't want it to get back to Cavo but he figured Lalonde would take Leslie out around the ninth round.

At the press conference, Stewart had said, "It would be better for Lalonde if the earth opened up and swallowed him before Sunday." There were fifteen thousand people in the stands who were glad that had not happened. They were ready to see the home boy lay on a whipping. All three preliminaries went the distance, and it was like suffering through two tumbling acts and an Italian mouse on "The Ed Sullivan Show" before Elvis came out.

After the last prelim, a gofer held up a large circular thermometer so that the CBS camera could get a shot of the needle nudging past 110°F. Then from the distance came the sound of drums, a vague thumping for a moment before you could pick out the beat. There was a rippling movement in the crowd, like a snake coming through tall grass. It was Stewart and his entourage, bobbing in a conga line, accompanied by steel drums to the ring. Held aloft over the challenger's head was a banner: "Sweeter than Sugar, Greater than Ali, Badder than Hagler, Baddest of the Bad." Stewart was hoisted into the ring, and on tiptoes danced a wide circle while his people shook the banner and thousands cheered.

Lalonde made his way to the ring without ceremony.

It started. There was not much feeling out; the fighters traded punches from the opening bell. Lalonde, who is not supposed to have a left, was scoring with left hooks. Midway through the second round that big right hand of his took advantage of a lazy jab and Stewart dropped like his legs had been yanked from under him. He got up almost as quickly but with an entirely different expression on his face. He seemed to be trying to keep astonishment from overwhelming his mask of baleful invincibility. Stewart danced away to clear his head and kept his distance until the round was done.

The rounds were not announced by the usual long-legged, scantily-attired women who pranced, hips rolling, around the ring on stiletto heels as the crowd hooted. The crowd hooted all right, but derisively, at a black dwarf in filthy children's clothes who made an attempt to get around the middle of the ring before the one-minute rest period was done. The crowd would laugh as he tumbled over and dropped his sign. He had baby bowlegs that ended in tiny monstrous shoes, the heels and soles thick yet old and run-down, laces gone; his head belonged to a ghastly giant—lumpy forehead, bulging eyes, thick, root-like hooked nose and tiny, thin-lipped, almost prissy mouth. But most horrible of all was his expression, a maniacal determination to make his poor circuit at whatever cost, no matter what taunts were directed at him, no matter how they laughed. His numbered boards were stacked near ringside and as each round ended he was shoved into action by a black man in a dashiki. This man would tease him, tell him the wrong number, then laugh at his confusion and look around at his companions for confirmation of the big joke. There were East Indians sitting near me and they looked away from the spectacle.

At the beginning of the third, Stewart was landing his left jab until Donny scored with a couple of rights. Stewart came back with his own hard right, but Lalonde won the round on the strength of some big combinations in the final seconds. The fourth round was Stewart's best effort. The Trinidadian was landing the left, then hooking to Lalonde's body and getting the right in as well. As he always did when he was in trouble, Lalonde brought his right foot, his back one, forward, leaving himself squared away and consequently off balance. He insisted on keeping his left dangerously low, at nearly waist level, making himself an easy target. His corner was hollering at him but he wouldn't raise the left, or else his concentration was failing him under pressure.

Whatever Gallagher and Cassidy told him between rounds had its effect, because he came out a different fighter in the fifth, pounding Stewart with rights and combinations. I noticed that the sunlight was bisected by the roof of the grandstand, leaving the ring neatly divided into equal triangles of intense light and softer shade. Lalonde stayed in the shade but near the border, with Stewart remaining in the sun. Lalonde crossed over only when Stewart threatened to encroach on his territory. A minute into the round Lalonde dropped his challenger with one right hand. Stewart barely beat the count, shook his head that he wasn't hurt and nodded to Denkin. No sooner had the referee waved them together than Lalonde got Stewart against the ropes, crossing into the sunshine and unloading first combinations, upstairs and down, then relying on rights, one after another. Stewart was trapped and helpless. He took ten unanswered blows to the head, only the ropes keeping him up. Denkin, who had been staring into Stewart's eyes the whole time, finally stepped in, waving Lalonde away. It was all over. Denkin held the challenger in his arms, and along with Stewart's handlers, helped him back to his stool.

The crowd sat in silence, not yet prepared to believe what had taken place. They remained in their seats until the official announcement. Only when Lalonde's hand was raised in victory by the referee did the crowd begin to move. Lalonde was carried out on the shoulders of his people. Stewart slumped on his stool as doctors looked into his eyes.

I wondered how that disc jockey was going to explain things to his listeners the next day.

There were a couple of hundred people milling around outside Lalonde's dressing-room door. Among them was the young black guy I had seen at the workout, the lone Lalonde supporter, who was now reminding everyone he had told them so. Every time the door opened to let somebody into the dressing room, the guy poked his head in to sing, "Don-nee! Don-nee!" The winner and still champion was sitting on a long, low bench having his hands unwrapped, breathing easily, looking as if he had just come in from a pleasant jog around the park. He said that it wasn't a consummate job of work he had performed out there. "I wasn't as good as I was against Davis when I was here the last time. I wasn't flowing. I was forcing it too much." A reporter from Toronto asked him whether he was surprised at how things had gone. Lalonde looked at him for a moment. I noticed that those blue eyes didn't change. His lips might turn down in a frown or up in a smile but the look in his eyes was constant. "Yes," Lalonde said. "I was surprised he kept getting up."

The names of possible future opponents were being tossed around by David Wolf. Hagler, Hearns and Leonard, primarily. It was then I noticed some people of indefinable race in expensive tropical-weight suits come into the dressing room. They were not part of the fight crowd; they were not local; they were representatives of the internationally wealthy. The world was soon going to change entirely for Donny Lalonde.

I rode back to the hotel with Citro and Cassidy. They discussed the mistakes Lalonde had made, and there had been plenty. Citro seemed amazed that anyone could violate all the fundamentals the way Donny did and still win. Failing to come up with any tangible explanation for the victory—it transcended merely the right hand—Citro fell back on the mystical, "He does it with pure heart." "Yeah, and balls," Cassidy added.

A month later I had lunch with Lalonde in a Winnipeg restaurant. We spoke of his upcoming fight with Sugar Ray Leonard, soon to be announced; about investments—he had just that morning bought a piece of land he hoped to turn into a golf course, acting—he had a part as a preacher in an upcoming movie, and music—just the week before he had met Bob Dylan. But no matter what the subject, the expression in his eyes remained the same. Flat.

Lalonde was in the middle of an explanation of why he didn't eat anything but fibre until noon when I realized who else had eyes like that. The other guy had been an enforcer for the mob. His name was Cecil Kirby and he later turned, gave evidence to the Crown, and wrote a book about his experiences. We had become acquaintances for various reasons. Kirby had the same blue eyes and the same steady look in them, a calm that was almost eerie because it masked and kept under control both a propensity for violence and a tremendous hurt. One of these two men was, of course, a bad man, the other a good man. But the look was the same.

The Prince and the Pauper

In the autumn of 1984, long before Michael Olajide, Jr., departed this country to try and take Manhattan, a magazine editor saw a newspaper photograph of the middleweight boxer and gave me a call. "This fellow, uh, Olla-jiddy, do you know anything about him?"

"Oh-*la*-jah-day? Saw him fight a couple of years ago. He won a decision over an American guy but got knocked down twice. Trained by his father. Seemed to have potential but needed lots of experience. The rap is he has a glass jaw. Another thing . . . "

"Never mind the sports stuff. I saw his picture and he's a handsome young man. Looks like Michael Jackson. Maybe that means there's a story."

So down I went to a spa over a disco on Vancouver's Hornby Street and found Junior doing calisthenics in the midst of a few white stock-market types. He appeared bigger and much more powerful than the skittish fighter I had watched in 1982.

I introduced myself to his father, who was overseeing the exercises with his right eye while his left one focussed elsewhere. Senior weighed about the same 160 pounds but was four inches shorter than his son's six feet. He spoke with the rhythms of Nigeria and old tribal tattoos had not faded from his forearms. He said that he had been taken advantage of in a business deal and was, thus, separated from his Kingsway Boxing Club on south Main Street. He called time to Junior and waved him over.

The kid looked only slightly more like Michael Jackson than I do. He didn't much resemble his father either. I was put in mind of an archaeological find made at Ibadan in southern Nigeria in the fifties. There they dug up heads of a sort of king-god called Shango who, it is believed, was a derivation of Amun, the Egyptian meteorite god. Junior had an Egyptian cast to his features, looks that back in Nigeria would have set him aside for special things. It soon became apparent that Junior considered himself a prince, at least, among ordinary folk.

We talked as Senior taped the fighter's hands. Junior was pleasant and friendly, self-possessed and frankly pleased at the prospect of publicity. He spoke well and was evidently as confident here as inside the ring. Every so often one of the half-dozen businessmen glanced our way. I got the impression that this kid could, should he wish, make a go at whatever it was any of them did. In other words, he didn't remind me of a fighter until he started pounding away at a heavy bag suspended from a whitewashed rafter in the club's laundry room. His left hooks made smacking dents from which the bag was slow to recover. His father grinned, "And Junior isn't even considered a puncher. He is more of a boxer. I've moulded him that way. Using my own experience to help him."

Most of what I knew about the Olajides concerned Senior, whose personality was assessed by local sports reporters and the fight mob as ranging over the entire terrain from difficult to impossible. But at our initial meeting he had not a bad word for anyone, not even members of the media. "The papers have said bad things about us," he shrugged, "but I would think everybody in town would work together to make a better situation for boxing."

About a month later, the Canadian Boxing Federation announced that its middleweight champion, Alex Hilton, would have to defend his Canadian title against number-one-ranked challenger Michael Olajide by the following January 25 or it would strip Hilton of said honour. That evening I telephoned the Olajides and got Junior, who said, "You better speak to my father."

The father said, "Alex Hilton and his people are afraid to fight us." Whether he believed this or not is irrelevant. The statement was stone boxing talk, best taken as: "Byzantine is the route these negotiations are taking."

In need of a guide through territory like this, I called Dave Brown. Brown, a former fighter, was then, and still is, the B.C. athletic commissioner. As such, he must see and approve all contracts. He is a short, compact, affable, white-haired man with a countenance that attests to the "pug" in pugilism. He had to that point refereed eight of Junior's twelve bouts. "Well, as for the kid fighting Alex Hilton, let me tell you that a few days ago Jack Spitzer, the leading promoter in Montreal, called asking me to relay an offer to the Olajides—he can't communicate with Senior. To fight Alex, Spitzer was offering $3000 and tickets plus $20,000 if Junior wins. So I told Senior, and got the usual answer: 'No way. They need us more than we need them.' " That $3000 may not even be chump change to the Junior of the big time and the big town today, but back then it happened to be $500 more than Olajide, hardly known east of New Westminster, had ever gotten for a fight.

But this was just so much annoying gorse—ahead lay thickets of brambles, maddening jungles, forbidding rain forests and deserts of deceit, not to mention a slough or two of despond and an occasional reward of peculiar vistas, like the first sight of Palenque, say, or a deserted principality designed by Piranesi. I skirted the gorse, detouring to the Astoria Hotel which has a gym in the basement under the pub.

Outside a nearby coffee shop an attractive woman of about twenty years stood on the curb smiling lasciviously at traffic. She was not to be confused with the tall, thin Indian transvestite who that day was, as usual, working the south side of the street about a block to the east. The woman had on a white cashmere sweater that might have belonged to her much younger sister, seeing as it left a lot uncovered and accentuated the rest. She waved at cars with one hand and rubbed her smooth belly with the other.

The low-ceilinged cellar room where the fighters, mostly amateurs, trained seemed quaint after the action on the street outside. The Astoria Club was headquarters for Dale Walters, featherweight bronze medal winner at the '84 Olympics. Like Olajide Junior, Walters had his father for a trainer. The war had deprived Len Walters of his own Olympic opportunity. His fair-haired son resembled a tough cherub. Watching Dale, I realized that although he had the moves and the killer instinct there was something missing. It was like a pianist who had taken lessons all his life, was technically proficient but could not for the life of him play jazz, and would never swing no matter how much he wanted to (or his teacher wanted him to). I left after a quarter of an hour; the relentless futility of the scene depressed me so much that even East Hastings Street was a relief.

I got on a bus and walked to the back where, across from me, sat a Chinese girl and a tall, skinny, cocoa-coloured kid in running shoes and a black nylon warm-up suit. The girl said, "How's Michael?"

"I don't know. I don't see him any more."

"You don't, like, train together?"

"No." When the kid shook his head, his mass of gelled curls trembled like a tangle of black eels waking up. "It's because of his father. He only has time for Michael."

That little snatch of conversation struck a chord. The kid got off at the first stop past Main. Glancing out the window as the bus rolled on, I saw him carrying a gym bag, striding along in the direction of—it had to be—the Shamrock.

The next coincidence occurred a week later when I saw a photo of this kid in the sports pages. According to the story, his name was Tony Pep. He was Canada's number one featherweight contender—Featherweight? Was he really no more than 126 pounds? At six-one?—and he was managed by Tony Dowling, who just happened to be the archrival of Michael Olajide, Sr.

The Shamrock had recently changed management and undergone a clean-up and fix-up. The faded old fight posters had been discarded and the walls painted Chinese-rooming-house blue. The place was not what it used to be and soon it would not be at all. Fifty years of memories were about to be kayoed by the wrecker's ball.

Present were the usual gym rats, dreamers slapping at the heavy bags, guys striking poses and copping attitudes, and the ever-present diminutive Mad Dog Ortega. All these people came and went, now you see 'em now you don't, like the Marx Brothers eluding the cops and Margaret Dumont.

I was introduced to Pep, who was arguing boxing history

with Tom Coady, a square-jawed, Irish-born heavyweight coming off a victory in Seattle over a male stripper-turned-boxer. Pep went into the ring to spar. He had the appearance of a young colt, all limbs, but he used his reach effectively, confusing his shorter, heavier opponent with jabs upstairs and down. To be six feet, one inch and 126 pounds is not to carry any excess poundage, or even ounce-age. Pep was imitating the Tommy Hearns style but more closely resembled Panama Al Brown, the world's bantamweight champion back at the time the Shamrock was born. Brown may have been two inches shorter than Pep, but he only weighed 116. In the films you see him jab-jabbing and getting away, moving side to side and slipping punches.

Leon Grinshpun, who was training Pep at the time, volunteered that the kid had all the natural ability in the world. "If he dedicates himself he can go far. If he has any fault it is maybe that he is too cocky." Later, after spending some time with Pep, I realized that what Grinshpun and others called cockiness was an air of self-reliance earned the hard way. Given what he had come out of, if he hadn't been cocky Tony would have been defeated.

He was twenty back then at the end of 1984, and had been living on his own for five years, a ward of the Ministry of Human Resources. He grew up, raised himself, in Vancouver's East End. "I don't have any memories of my father," he told me. "My mother's last name was Pipke. When I was real little we lived in Seattle. I don't even know why we were there."

When he was ten years old, Tony watched his mother, a heroin addict, die of an overdose. "After that I lived in different group homes up here. But I was always running away. And I ran away from school too. They have these guys who drive around in cars looking for kids who aren't in school. And they always brought me back." Not surprisingly, he got into his share of trouble as a kid, often by stealing bicycles. "We sold them to a guy for money. When I was sixteen, MHR took me out of the group homes and put me up in an apartment of my own. They gave me food vouchers, too."

When you are a teenaged welfare case living on your own, what do you do with yourself? When you look like a product of your background are they going to give you a job at a fast food franchise? Do you go into crime? Get into boxing? Since the first option was ridiculous, Tony settled for the third, after another try at number two. Charged with possession of stolen goods, he looked to boxing for salvation. He also went back to school to get his diploma. One of his classmates was Michael Olajide. "I knew his father had a gym. So I went there."

After only a dozen amateur fights, and needing money, Tony turned pro under Mike Senior. "But I soon realized he only had time for Junior. I heard about the Shamrock and Tony Dowling." As well as gyms, he changed names, from Pipke to Pep, in homage to Willie Pep, probably the greatest of all featherweights.

Towards the end of January 1986, it became known that Alex, Matthew and Davey Hilton were about to sign promotional contracts with Don King. The electric-haired promoter was not about to permit Alex Hilton to fight anybody named Michael Olajide for something called the Canadian middleweight championship. The Canadian Boxing Federation responded to the imminent relationship by drawing itself up to full height and firing off a repeat of its threat to strip Hilton of his title. The trajectory of this salvo was a straight line ending in the vicinity of the Hilton shins. They signed anyway. In Vancouver, Mike Senior announced a press conference at the Hyatt Regency Hotel designed to ballyhoo Junior's bid for the now vacant championship against an opponent to be introduced that day. I have tried since then to decide which is more indicative of the health of boxing: that only three members of the media showed up for the press conference, or that neither Olajide, opponent or promoter put in an appearance.

Finally, an actual card was made, slated for April 11 at the

PNE Agrodome and billed as a Night of the Champions. Olajide and Wayne Caplette would vie for the middleweight title, Tony Pep and Nedrie Simmons, the featherweight.

Every morning at nine-thirty, Tony Pep would jog by my place in the east end and do a leisurely lap or two around the Britannia High School track. Some afternoons I went to the Shamrock to watch him train; he was there only occasionally. Once when he was not, his trainer, Grinshpun, threw out his hands as if tossing confetti at a wedding. "Tony, he is good boy but he has to take this fight seriously. In Russia fighters are dedicated. In Russia, this would not happen."

Due to a scheduling snafu, the date of the fight had to be set back one day, to April 10. Olajide Senior protested, demanding $2000 for the inconvenience. The commission told him to cooperate or take a hike. He cooperated.

He was not so cooperative with me, at least at first. The Olajides were back at the Kingsway Club, Senior evidently having straightened out his pecuniary disagreements. (He had told me somebody took advantage of him; his landlord said he didn't pay the rent.) The club was on the second floor of a building a few blocks down from a McDonald's in a neighbourhood that was just seeing the first antique shops of gentrification. Senior met me at the top of the stairs with news that I would not be permitted to come the rest of the way. "No visitors. We training in secret."

Next day at the Shamrock someone told me Senior had called and left word for me to come by. I would not have believed this except that there were two identical messages from him at home. So with the fight a week away, I returned to the Kingsway and Senior was again at the top of the stairs, this time like a maître d' exuding professional sincerity. "Come on up, come on in! I apologize, I apologize."

One ring, one heavy bag, one speed bag and one bench; no posters, card players, wise guys or hangers-on with ginger-root noses. The place looked as austere as a Methodist church. The bench was occupied by Junior's boom box and three teenaged girls who looked at him with idolatry whenever he came over to change the tape.

Over the next few days, I spoke with Senior a lot and Junior a little. The former would invite me into his office, closing the door and sitting at an old desk, the wall behind him filled with Junior's press clippings. The office seemed clean despite trash heaped methodically in pyramids in the corners.

Senior was born Ijero-Ekiti in Lagos. "As a child I was the only kid who would not fight. I always ran home. One day, a little girl beat me up. I went home and my mother was angry. She said, 'Take me to the house of the child who did this to you.' I took her, and the girl's mother came to the door. 'Your son beat up my son.' The lady said, 'But I have no son. I only have a daughter.' We went away in shame. My father, who was a gentle man, picked me up with one hand and told me he would give me a licking if this ever happened again. I then started taking boxing lessons."

He turned pro at fifteen and two years later signed a contract with George Beddles, manager of his hero, Hogan "Kid" Bassey. Olajide claims to have won the Nigerian and West African lightweight titles but my search of the records revealed that although he challenged for the British West African title, he lost to Floyd Robertson at Accra on March 8, 1958.

"I moved to England to fight and made trips to the States. There were never good enough opponents for me. I never got a shot at a championship although I was considered championship material. I was the number one Commonwealth contender. There was always politics involved, and wherever I went I was a foreigner." Again the records contradict his claims. The listings fail to show a top ten ranking for Olajide in either the Commonwealth or England. His record from 1958 through 1960 is seven wins, five losses and a draw.

"I am a good trainer because I try to get close to the kid, see what kind of personality he has. I motivate his dedication. If this is not the case, a fighter does not give respect to a trainer. That's the way it is with Dowling's fighters: there is no understanding there. I train the boy from the beginning. Those others, the Dowlings, they don't know anything. Even the famous ones, like Angelo Dundee and Eddie Futch. They are just caretakers. Only Emmanuel Stewart is as good a trainer as I am." (An article that appeared in *Boxing Review* magazine at this time did not share Olajide's regard for his own abilities. Olajide, it maintained, trained his fighters "to fight like bunny rabbits. They throw bunny rabbit punches.")

Mike Senior continued his rant against Dowling. "He is jealous of me because I have all the talent. He ruined Jamey Ollenberger. Look at the boy's face, all the scar tissue. Dowling's idea of training is to give a fighter whiskey between the rounds. As for working the corner, here's Dowling . . ." Olajide sprang to his feet, knocking back his chair. "Kill him!" he hollered, waving his arms in a hilarious imitation of Dowling. "Kill him! Kill him!"

A few days before the fight, driving down Main Street in the ten-year-old yellow family Fury, Michael echoed his father's ideas about dedication. "I am truly devoted to what I am doing. If my father wasn't involved, I'd be the same way. I don't drink or smoke dope, and I don't party till all hours and hang around with the kind of people that Tony Pep does." I mentioned that Pep had told me he still regarded Junior as his friend. "No, Tony Pep cannot be my son's friend," Senior responded. Junior nodded in agreement. "He's not my friend. Obviously if what he does doesn't set right with my father, it doesn't set right with me."

That day the Vancouver *Sun* ran an item that had the odour of a promoter's plant. Junior was beating up on his sparring partners with such ferocity, it asserted, that one of them, Roosevelt Green, had quit and gone home. The next day a story in *USA Today* said that Thomas Hearns, training for his fight with Marvin Hagler, had been beating up on his sparring partners with such ferocity that one of them, Roosevelt Green, had quit and gone home.

April 8: an actual press conference at the Sandman Hotel. The usual suspects were present, milling, to use a word of pugilistic etymology, in the Sportsline Lounge, sipping beer and eyeing the fried objects of unfathomable origin floating in the samovar. Bruce Allen, the music promoter, had joined Jack McLaughlin in staging the bout, and had Dale Walters making his pro debut on the card. Everywhere Allen went he was followed by a guy with long hair and a walkie-talkie stuck to his ear.

McLaughlin—large, aging, red-faced and phlegmatic—told me about what a great fight town Vancouver used to be in the 1940s and how, with the aid of cards like this, it could be again. Tony Dowling assured me he was well prepared for the fight. "I've bought a bottle of Bushmills for my boys."

The fighters were positioned behind a table, each with a hastily scrawled name card. Tony Pep, in red-and-white striped sweater, cream-coloured slacks and black shoes, thanked the promoters and vowed to do his best. Simmons, his shorter, darker opponent, solemnly promised a good fight.

Michael Olajide was tricked out in a white suit with red tie and pocket handkerchief, black cummerbund and black-and-grey lace-up, pointy-toed shoes. As he reached inside his jacket pocket, you just knew that Michael was about to take his place in the long, long list of scribbling scufflers. He produced a folded sheet of notebook paper and began to intone couplets prophesying a kayo in four.

Boxing fans raised on Muhammad Ali's verse are unaware that the tradition goes back forever, or at least to an era when fights might last all day, and thus fittingly inspired epics rather than mere ditties. George Borrow, an English writer of the mid–nineteenth century, was as fanatical about boxing as about other things. (Borrow once hitched a pair of mules to a wagon, loaded the wagon with Bibles and set off for Barcelona, possessed of the thoroughly ridiculous notion of selling Bibles to gypsies. He may be credited with the dubious distinction of introducing prize fighting to Spain; all that one hundred and fifty years of evolution has produced is Alfredo Evangelista.) Borrow happened to be in a tavern on the eve of the Jem Mace-Bill Thorpe fight as the Nonpareil Jem cleared his throat, drained his glass and set off on a bout of truly epic versifying—much of it recorded by Borrow—that ended with the poetic peroration: "Thus surely shall I dispatch him to heaven, / Long about the round forty-seven."

In modern times, Philadelphia Jack O'Brien, a literary and elocutionary influence on W. C. Fields, composed roundels; that Shakespearean scholar, Gene Tunney, sonnets. There was even a pretty good middleweight out of New Jersey by the name of Teddy Mann who claimed Kerouac as his literary champ. Once, during a television interview after he had taken a tough decision in Atlantic City, Mann said hello to his parents, then launched into a paragraph from *Doctor Sax*. The interviewer cut him off a couple of sentences into it, evidently concluding that such mumbo jumbo might lend ammunition to those who claim boxing causes brain damage.

As for Junior, he tended to telegraph his strophes; otherwise it was decent, serviceable verse no worse, and certainly more lively, than Margaret Atwood's. His opponent Wayne Caplette, in T-shirt and cap, smiled beneath his moustache. More the prose type, he allowed as how Mr. Olajide was in for a surprise.

Fight night at the Agrodome. The bell for the featherweight championship of Canada. Pep is visibly nervous. Simmons wastes little time, connecting with a couple of left hooks that send Pep to the ropes. Pep survives but he is lunging with his jab, thus nullifying his reach advantage, allowing Simmons to get inside. By the time the jab lands—if it lands—it is about as effective as a nudge from the balloon gloves of a cartoon palooka.

There are tactical problems for each fighter. Pep loosens up enough to keep Simmons away but it becomes apparent he is stymied by his opponent's left-handed stance and, thus, is unable to score. Simmons, in turn, is obviously frustrated at not being able to reach Pep. Not realizing that a mental battle is taking place, certain members of the crowd begin to boo a perceived lack of action.

Pep, who has never gone beyond eight rounds, gets stronger. Entering the eleventh, championship territory, he gets Simmons and unleashes a furious combination that almost puts his opponent away. Again and again, Pep scores with the right, having figured out that Simmons, like many southpaws, is vulnerable to it after throwing a jab. At the end of the fight it seems clear that Pep has won the last eight rounds, albeit narrowly. Two judges vote for him, one for Simmons. The crowd boos. Not because it is a split decision, but because Pep has won. Save for a welt under his left eye, Pep is unmarked. Simmons goes to the hospital.

The main event: With little fanfare, Caplette attains the ring and discards his robe, revealing a body white as a fish's belly. He has a tattoo. His back is rounded, almost humped. He should have kept his robe on, because Olajide is going to make him wait.

After several minutes, there is Michael Jackson's "Thriller." Olajide makes the walk in the midst of his entourage, which looks like the multiracial cast of a McDonald's commercial. Olajide dances around the ring in red-and-white trunks, shoes, tassels. He tosses his pomaded locks, goes over to Caplette's corner, smirks and glides away. Caplette glances at him, bemused.

Not much of the first round goes by before Caplette's nose is reddened. In the second, Olajide reveals a disastrous tendency to jump back from a punch with his hands away from his face. In the third, after taking some punishment in the clinches, Olajide knocks Caplette to the canvas and stands over him wiggling his hips. Beginning in round five, Caplette's upper-balcony fans begin counting the rounds out loud to taunt Olajide. "Whatever happened to five, Michael?"

Throughout the fight it has become apparent that Olajide does not like the rough in-fighting, would rather not be anywhere near the ropes. Then comes the controversial ninth round. For the first two-and-a-half minutes Caplette is taking a beating. Suddenly a white towel sails into the ring from his corner. Caplette's trainer, Peter Piper, climbs onto the ring apron, apparently to stop the fight. But only referee Barney O'Connor has that power. O'Connor separates the fighters and looks to the trainer, but Piper says nothing and begins to turn away. O'Connor calls the fighters back together. Caplette, who appears confused, fails to put up his guard and Olajide socks him. Caplette goes down hard and Olajide raises his arms in victory. The crowd responds with vociferous booing.

Things look like turning nasty when dissatisfied customers rush to the ring hollering abuse at Olajide, who has done nothing technically wrong. Caplette was obliged to protect himself at all times. After the official decision is given by the ring announcer, Olajide remains in the centre of the ring for the benefit of the video cameras and probably his own safety. By the time he climbs out of the ring several minutes later, the scene has cooled. His face is unmarked, his gleaming smile back in place. He is greeted by groupies in "The Silk" T-shirts.

After the decision is announced I see Tony Pep get up from his ringside seat and head for the dressing room, minus an entourage. But waiting for him by the doors, staring out at the rain, is a woman in a clinging knit dress and stiletto heels. She has black Prince Valiant hair, speaks with a Nordic accent, and is at least ten years older than Pep. She is not the type you find at McDonald's.

Olajide was back at the PNE Agrodome a few days later for the closed-circuit broadcast of the Hagler-Hearns fight. He was dressed to the nines, working the crowd and regally accepting congratulations. After the main event, one of the most exciting bouts in memory, Olajide responded to a newspaper reporter's query by saying that, given a year of seasoning, he'd be ready to take away Hagler's world middleweight title.

The day before the broadcast, up at Broadway and Commercial, I had seen Tony Pep waiting for the bus in the rain.

So there were now two new Canadian champs, for what it was worth. It was worth nothing in their own hometown. One of the local papers had responded to their triumphs with the headline, "Night of the Chumps."

There was some uninformed talk of Olajide fighting one of the Hiltons but that wasn't going to happen. Michael travelled instead to the boxing-mad island nation of Fiji to take an easy victory from a local fellow. In Winnipeg, Pep scored a first-round knockout over a dangerously overmatched little guy named Clint Hannah.

Walking into a boxing banquet in Burnaby, I was immediately aware of being the object of two distinct sets of hostile looks. They emanated from different parts of the room, but from the same family. A couple of minutes later, turning from the table of cold cuts and celery stalks spread with cream cheese, I still felt Junior's eyes. They were, to paraphrase the old expression, "shooting daggers": there was a jab in one, an uppercut in the other. I went over and he continued to stare, paying no attention to the fellow who was talking to him. "I didn't like the way you treated me in that article," he said finally, continuing to give the bad glare, leaving unspoken the fact that he was probably considering the implications of separating my head from the rest of me. Junior, and his looks, had inspired the article, which was published in a Vancouver magazine. I had also brought Tony Pep into it, contrasting the lives of the two fighters.

I was aware that the other person had trailed off in midsentence and sort of backed away. For a moment I actually thought Michael was going to get physical. I could just see the headline, "21-Year-Old Champ Kayoes Middle-Aged Writer." Maybe he was thinking, "I'd really like to hurt him a little but there might be all these messy ramifications so perhaps I could just get in one short little dig to his midsection and nonchalantly drift away in search of a light beer as if nothing had happened."

I asked him what hadn't pleased him.

"You made Tony Pep out to be some romantic figure."

"I should have made *you* out to be the romantic figure?"

His expression said, "*Well . . .*" Then he looked away and came back with, "And you made it seem like my father was my boss."

"I'm pretty sure everything I wrote was the truth. I didn't misquote either of you, did I?"

His eyes seemed to crackle. There was lots of white around the pupils. "My father didn't like it either."

So I went to confront Senior, who told me, "You should say only good things." He stared at me too, but it was a flat stare with no uncertainty behind it, mind made up. In the 4:00 A.M. back alley of the soul, I wouldn't want to meet the old man. I'd rather run into Junior, who might be susceptible to some psychic trick. As for Senior, you might as well try conning a pit bull. Funny thing, though. After a couple of minutes, Senior smiled as if he meant it. Truth was, he probably enjoyed the role in which he'd been cast; it fit like Svengali's cape.

The Olajides took their act to New York at the end of 1986, immediately announcing their intention of being known as the best fighter and the best trainer in the world. Word travelled back over the grapevine that New York considered Junior to have possibilities but the old man had to go. In the next year and a half, Junior commanded a lot of press attention as a model and would-be actor. His boxing career—he beat Curtis Parker and James Green—seemed almost incidental. Then, in his television debut on NBC, he knocked out tough veteran Don Lee in the ninth round and became an instant media darling.

Meanwhile, Tony Pep had a few fights, mostly against nonentities; his most impressive win came against Ian Clyde in Montreal. While the Vancouver papers made no mention of that fight, they did devote space to an unscheduled encounter of Pep's that occurred in a supermarket. Pep interrupted a spirited argument with his girl friend to deal with a man who had taken it upon himself to intercede. The guy was taken to hospital with a broken jaw.

Pep managed to avoid a jail sentence, and was equally successful at avoiding training. When he did show up, he seemed to just go through the motions. He had a fight in Australia and was robbed of a decision. Maybe the injustice of it soured Pep, but his lack of inclination probably had deeper roots. It appeared, to me anyway, that he thought his victories would be diminished if he put himself out by training and clean living. Nothing could be cooler than winning without pushing. It was a street attitude, and he was nothing if not a corner boy.

But Tony was a complicated kid, and God knows what demons were at work in his mind. He rose to the occasion when sent to Ireland as a sparring partner for the popular lightweight champion Barry McGuigan but he wanted no part of a match with Azumah Nelson, the featherweight champion from Ghana who many considered the most skilled fighter in the world. He seemed to sleepwalk through most of his November 1986 bout with Dale Walters, finally coming to in the tenth to knock out the former bronze medallist.

Meanwhile Junior was modelling for *Ebony* and being featured in American boxing publications. He was interviewed, along with his father, by *KO* magazine, where the following exchange was published in July 1987:

KO: Do you two ever argue about anything having to do with boxing?

Junior: Maybe little things, but nothing big. I always lose the arguments anyway (*laughs*).

Senior: One of the things about being a fighter myself . . .

when he first started out he might have took certain things and said, "I want to do it this way." I said, "Look, I will step in the ring with you. If you can get away with the move you are trying to use and not get hit, you can use it."

Junior: I was only a junior welterweight then (*laughs*). (*Senior, not amused, shoots a quick glance at his son.*)

Junior: I'm only joking (*laughs*).

In October 1987, Olajide met Frank Tate at Caesar's Palace for the vacant International Boxing Federation middleweight title. Although Tate had won the middleweight gold at the '84 Olympics, Olajide was more popular. Tate, a workmanlike, unexciting fighter, was no match in the charisma department for fashion-plate Michael Junior. It was billed as a classic boxer-puncher confrontation. But Tate did not follow the script; he refused to wait for his cues, stole scenes and outboxed the boxer. After losing the decision, Michael claimed he was tired from overtraining.

Usually the division with the most talented boxers, the middleweight firmament was not shining very brightly at the time. Hagler, though not officially retired, had been inactive since his loss to Sugar Ray Leonard a year earlier. Michael Nunn, the rising star, had not yet begun to glitter. As for Tate, he never would. As months went by and the middleweight heaven remained dim, it was decided to relight Michael Junior. Thus, after a couple of tune-up fights, he was given a chance at rugged Iran Barkley. Barkley was regarded as a throwback to an era when men fought now extinct animals with clubs. During interviews, Olajide grimaced at the mention of his opponent's name, pretending to be horrified by Barkley's looks. Olajide called him "Plunger Lips."

Barkley replied, "He's cute. He's in the wrong business. He should put on a skirt."

He stopped Olajide in the fifth.

But Barkley went nowhere after that fight, and the middleweight division followed. Over the next couple of years, the only fights that garnered any interest were those featuring old warriors like Leonard and Hearns, and even that old, blown-up lightweight Roberto Duran. Leonard and Duran fought for the third time in a sad travesty of their June 1980 bout; Duran won. The Panamanian with the hands of stone quit the ring five months later in the rematch, uttering those now immortal words, "No más." After their third bout, the unanimous verdict was "Nada más."

Leonard and Hearns fought a rematch delayed nine years in a bout billed as Geezers at Caesar's. But at least people showed up, as they would not for anything involving the other middleweights. Hearns earned a draw, though most people thought he'd won. The Hit Man came away with the public's acknowledgement and was inspired to fight again. There was only one person he could fight on television and that was Michael Olajide, Jr., resurrected once again.

The Hit Man evidently regarded their April 28, 1990, bout as a steppingstone to heavier divisions. He was actually talking about moving on to cruiserweight and even heavyweight. This kind of talk furnished the only reason for betting on Olajide; you had to surmise that Tommy's senses had been scrambled.

But, of course, anything can happen in boxing. After all, Junior and Senior had split up. The parting was acrimonious. For the Hearns bout, Junior was being trained by Angelo Dundee, and how galling that must have been for Senior, who considered Dundee a mere "caretaker." Reporters noted that Olajide had shown ability as a model, an actor and an author of children's books as well as a prize fighter. Emmanuel Stewart, Hearns's trainer, said that Tommy was going to help Olajide make a career decision by eliminating boxing as a viable source of endeavour.

The fight inaugurated the Trump Taj Mahal in Atlantic City. Olajide said he was really serious; hence his new short haircut. The maharajah was going to get down from the litter. So he said. Actually, he came out nervous as a new colt, tentative, as he had been with Tate, with Barkley, as he had been way back in 1982 against Stacy McSwain. In the early rounds, Hearns taunted Michael Junior, measuring the other boxer, wiggling his hips, dropping his hands in disdain. Olajide had done much the same things once with Wayne Caplette. It was not until the ninth round when Hearns knocked him to the canvas that Olajide showed any aggressiveness. Getting to his feet, he stood and traded with the Hit Man, backing him up against the ropes. In the tenth, Olajide scored with a combination that caused Hearns to wobble. But he couldn't capitalize on the damage. The fight went the distance and everybody was surprised that Olajide was there for the final bell.

Hearns's excuse was that his mind hadn't been all there, the implication being that he had been looking ahead to greater things. Boxing people had expected an inevitable knockout that would put an end to Olajide's career but now that it hadn't come, they were intimating it was farewell to Hearns. The feeling was that if he couldn't put Olajide away, he might as well give it up. Ironically, going the distance with wobbly Tommy would probably ensure Junior of one more respectable payday. For this one, he had earned a quarter of a million dollars.

Earlier that same week, far away from the Taj Mahal, Tony Pep fought a scheduled six-rounder in Red Deer, Alberta. He stopped an opponent named Tony Cisneros from Phoenix in the second. His paycheque was $249,000 less than Michael Olajide's.

Kid Celluloid

There I was talking to Gorbachev one day in 1984 when who should lumber over but Richie Giachetti. Gorbachev had a birthmark on the top of his head like a splattering of fuchsia paint; Giachetti had a scar bisecting his cheek like a knife wound, which it was. "Sly," Giachetti said, "says to tell you you look good in the rushes."

Richie Giachetti was real, but Gorby was an impostor, and we were on the set of *Rocky IV*. The company was filming the climactic fight scene at the PNE Agrodome in Vancouver. I was employed for two weeks as what is called an SOC, a silent-on-camera, a sort of glorified extra. I was a KGB thug in an old-fashioned double-breasted suit, clothes deemed appropriate for contemporary U.S.S.R. When Rocky Balboa entered the arena filled with thousands of whistling Muscovites—whistling is the Russian version of booing, it was explained—I was to step from my front-row seat, block his path momentarily and shake my fist at him. Later, after he whipped poor Drago, I rushed into the ring, grabbed Rocky B. and spun him around on my shoulders. Alas—familiar story—my big scenes did not appear in the version shown in North American release. I know I made the TV ads for the film as well as the video version, because I went into a bar in Zihuatanejo, Mexico, one time when *Rocky IV* was on the television. There was a Mexican guy in there who looked like a smaller version of Richie Giachetti. He glanced at me, up at the screen, back at me, then smiled like Eli Wallach smiles in *The Professionals* when he announces to the gringos that he and his pals are not murderous, thieving cutthroats but just poor simple peasants.

I knew Giachetti, then Larry Holmes's trainer and later to be Mike Tyson's, from his trips to Vancouver and had spent some time with him in Las Vegas when Gordy Racette fought Tony Tubbs. His job on the movie was to choreograph the fight scenes and to act as a general boxing adviser. It was curious to see a man who was a big deal in big-time boxing filling this relatively inferior position. When Richie told Larry Holmes to do something, the then heavyweight champion of the world obeyed. Not so Sylvester Stallone.

A lot of idle moments, of which there were plenty, were spent talking with Richie. Maybe I was supposed to ask him for an introduction to Stallone, but I didn't. Occasionally, during a setup, the star would take a short walk without his bodyguards along the perimeter of the set, his head bent in concentration. No one said anything to him then. A few times he looked sideways at me out of curiosity. Giachetti had no doubt told him I was the guy who had written a piece for a Vancouver magazine about Gordy Racette and Tiger Eye, Stallone's boxing outfit.

On this particular afternoon there was a camera change that took a good half-hour, as carpenters scurried about and gofers searched for Stallone's star filter. Returning from the coffee urn, I heard Brigitte Nielsen saying to her stand-in, with much exasperation, "Sly kept waking me up all night complaining about a pain in his chest. I was furious. I need my sleep!" (Stallone had ripped a chest muscle pulling up on one of his haymakers.) I returned to my seat in the now empty front row. Giachetti and Stallone were talking nearby, and the star turned and walked in my direction. He took a seat to my left, leaving three vacant seats between us. His bodyguard was posted near the ring, about forty feet away. Stallone was wearing only his boxing trunks, white socks and white boxing shoes. He was deeply tanned, having just returned from Thailand and the filming of a Rambo movie. There was none of the bulk of the bodybuilder to him but his muscles were highly defined. He looked like some guy I might have grown up with in South Philadelphia which was, in fact, where Rocky Balboa lived, but Stallone himself had been raised in a well-off section of North Philadelphia, had gone to private school and played polo. The only times any of *us* had been on a horse were when the old Italian came around the neighbourhood carrying a camera and leading a Shetland pony. Every living room in South Philadelphia had a framed photo on top of the television set of a kid on a Shetland pony.

I was obviously supposed to say something to him. But I didn't want to say something stupid like, "Yo, I come from Balboa's neighbourhood," and Gordy Racette was a sore point. I heard that he had seen a lot of boxing movies prior to making his own so I said, "*The Set Up*, great movie. I wonder if you ever saw that?"

His arms were thrown back over the seats on either side of him. He turned his head and looked at me; he was surprised but wasn't going to let it show. "Robert Ryan was tremendous. Everything shot at night."

"Perfect film noir."

"Yeah, sometimes I think, if I do another *Rocky*, I'll wind it up like that. Back on the street where it all began."

Stallone said that Ryan, indeed, most of the actors in the classic boxing films, guys like Garfield, Holden, Kirk Douglas, had all been out of shape, a fact that made it difficult to take the films seriously. From there we had a brief discussion of how Rocky Balboa would have fared against other cinematic pugilists: Stoker (Ryan) in *The Set Up*; Newman as Rocky Graziano in *Somebody Up There Likes Me*; Quisenberry (Wayne Morris) in the original *Kid Galahad*; Charley (Garfield) in *Body and Soul*. It was fun—for a while.

There have been far more movies made about boxing than about any other sport. Not only was the first sports film a boxing movie, the first commercially successful motion pictures were of actual bouts. Thomas Edison is usually credited with making the first boxing film, of a fight between Gentleman Jim Corbett and Peter Courtney staged at Edison's studio in West Orange, New Jersey, in September 1894. Actually, another film had been shown six weeks earlier in New York. This was a fight between lightweights Michael Leonard and Jack Cushing. The bout was to last ten rounds for the benefit of moviegoers but Leonard got carried away and kayoed Cushing with a right to the jaw in the sixth. Both these films had been made to be viewed through a peephole apparatus. The third fight film, *Young Griffo and Battling Barnett*, was the first motion picture to be seen on a large screen. The first theatre presentation of a full-length movie of any kind, November 21, 1899, was the James J. Jeffries-Tom Sharkey fight. It lasted twenty-five rounds, with an intermission for vaudeville acts.

Several founders of Vitagraph, Selig and Essanay, the pioneering film companies in New York, had sporting connections. Max Aronson, the first western star, promoted fights under the name Bronco Billy Anderson. William S. Hart used his movie earnings to buy the Western Athletic Club, the most popular fight arena in Los Angeles. Tom McCarey, the leading fight promoter on the west coast, was the father of two successful directors, Leo and Roger McCarey. Mack Sennett was a regular at Kid McCoy's Manhattan saloon, as was David Wark Griffith.

McCoy was a boyish-looking fighter who was born Norman Selby. He left his real identity back on the Indiana farm he fled in the 1880s. He engaged in hundreds of professional fights, from the lightweight division to the heavyweight, and the first time the expression "best fighter pound for pound" was used it was to compliment the Kid. In fact, McCoy fought so often and at so many weights that other fighters had no qualms about billing themselves as Kid McCoy in order to enhance their value. After one of Selby's battles with heavyweight Joe Choynski, a sportswriter began his story, "Now you've seen the Real McCoy." Thus was born a phrase that came to mean "authentic," "the genuine article." Ironically, McCoy was not the man's real name, and the man himself would later, and repeatedly, be brought up on criminal charges ranging from diamond smuggling to murder. The Kid had quite a career. He once lived with the Nobel Prize winner Maurice Maeterlinck, at the time the most famous author in the world. D. W. Griffith had the Kid give him boxing lessons, and when the director made *Broken Blossoms* he used McCoy in the great fight scene with Donald Crisp. McCoy went on to other small acting jobs, but his greatest contribution to drama was his own life. The Kid was played on Broadway by Lionel Barrymore in *The Wrong Girl.* The Kid's story launched Barrymore in much the same manner that Rocky Graziano's would make a star of Paul Newman sixty years later.

There were hundreds of silent-screen films and hundreds more boxing talkies. It is a subject that has engaged the interest of the greatest directors: Alfred Hitchcock, Charlie Chaplin, Rouben Mamoulian, Robert Wise, King Vidor, John Huston, Luchino Visconti, Martin Scorsese. Hitchcock's *The Ring* was called "the most magnificent film ever made" when it was released in 1927.

Name a great actor from the past and chances are good he played a fighter or fight manager at least once during his career. Buster Keaton? He was a spoiled little rich boy turned boxer in *Battling Butler*. Chaplin? Several times, beginning with *The Knockout*, a Keystone two-reeler in which Charlie referees a bout between Fatty Arbuckle and Edgar Kennedy. John Wayne? The Duke was a lumberjack turned boxer in *Conflict*, but is best remembered for his role in the 1952 film *The Quiet Man*, in which he plays an American who returns to his ancestral Irish home after killing a man in the ring in Pittsburgh. He refuses to fight the bullying Victor McLaglen until his own wife, Maureen O'Hara, who is also Victor's sister, calls him a coward. There ensues the longest, and the most boring, fight ever filmed. McLaglen, the former heavyweight challenger, was sixty-seven years old at the time but still had some good moves. In *From Here to Eternity*, Montgomery Clift had blinded a man in the ring and refused to fight again. Clark Gable was the heavyweight champion of the world in the comedy *Cain and Mabel*. Burt Lancaster appeared in *The Killers*, a film very loosely based on the Hemingway story. In *Here Comes Mr. Jordan* (1941), Robert Montgomery dies in a plane crash before he has a chance to become the light heavyweight champ. (The film was remade as *Heaven Can Wait* in 1978, with Warren Beatty as a football player.) Elvis Presley was *Kid Galahad* in the 1962 remake of the 1930s original that starred Wayne Morris as the bellhop with the kayo punch and Edward G. Robinson as his manager. Errol Flynn was James J. Corbett in *Gentleman Jim* (1942), one of the best boxing movies ever made.

There have been some extremely unlikely cinematic sluggers too, such as Danny Kaye, delightful as the coward who turns tiger and wins the middleweight championship (and Virginia Mayo) in *The Kid from Brooklyn*. In 1936's *The Milky Way*, Harold Lloyd was a fighting milkman who didn't remove his glasses in the ring. Mickey Rooney's first adult role was as the eponymous *Killer McCoy*. In *Palooka*, Stuart Erwin was a rather ridiculous Joe Palooka with Jimmy Durante as Knobby, his manager. Even Rock Hudson was a boxer; in *Iron Man*, he and Jeff Chandler play two fighters nicknamed Coke and Speed.

Rarely has the action in a boxing movie been restricted to the squared circle. Behind the battling bruisers stand the mugs, thugs, broken-down pugs, flimflam men and floozies. Compared to many of the fight films that went before, Stallone's Rocky series seems grounded in reality. The first one, in fact, was inspired by the story of Chuck Wepner, "the Bayonne Bleeder," a New Jersey club fighter who decked Muhammad Ali before going down to defeat.

The idea of a deaf-mute boxer having his speech and hearing restored by just the right shot to the head seems far-fetched, but it happened to one Danny London in real life and to Tony Curtis in *Flesh and Fury*. Curtis also appeared in *The Square Jungle* in 1955, with Ernest Borgnine as his Shakespeare-quoting trainer. William Holden has to postpone his promising career as a violinist to earn money to escape the slums in *Golden Boy*. "Feelings" should have been the theme song of this one; Holden has too many of them to be a good boxer. His hands are just as sensitive as the rest of him. He breaks them, and surely will never play the violin again despite the soothing assurances of his girl friend Barbara Stanwyck.

Then there was always some guy like Cagney, a poor slob who never had a chance. His brother has the brains in the family, what it takes to escape the tenements and even, maybe, someday give a piano recital at Carnegie Hall. The whole family has to scrape and scuffle for every dime, especially since the old man caught a side-door Pullman after a Bowery binge and hasn't been heard from since. Cagney is just smart enough to know he's not smart enough to be any more than a pug, so he laces on the gloves to pay for his brother's music lessons. Finally he's doing something decent with his life, and what happens? He is blinded when an opponent rubs resin in his eyes. From then on it's a newsstand on the corner for Cagney, whose face breaks into a beatific smile when he hears his brother's recital broadcast on the radio. This is the actual plot of *City for Conquest*, released in 1940.

Cagney might have copped out on the side of Good and Right during the last moments of *Public Enemy* as he walked Spanish from his cell to the electric chair, but he would have socked anyone who hinted he should take a dive. Attempts to get a boxer to go in the tank became standard in fight films. Usually the central character was forced to take the fall, criminal managers and the mob being behind it all. "You're going to get caught with a big right hand in the eighth round, see?"

"Not me! What'd you think I am, some chump you can boss around?"

"You got a real pretty girl friend, don't you?"

"What of it?"

"You ever seen what happens to a pretty girl friend, she accidentally gets acid thrown in her face?"

Dives not taken are the subject of both the classic boxing movie *Body and Soul* and *The Set Up*, the greatest boxing movie ever made. *Body and Soul* has the dark, brooding photography of James Wong Howe and the dark, existential brooding of John Garfield. Directed by Robert Rossen, the film starts out with Garfield as a young Jewish corner boy. For the hell of it, he enters an amateur boxing contest. He wins. Then he meets Lilli Palmer, an uptown artist who is the feminine representative of a world he could heretofore only imagine. Garfield turns pro to save his mother from poverty after the death of his old man. He rises rapidly through the ranks, winning twenty-one fights, nineteen by knockout. He's after the big bucks, so he hooks up with a crooked promoter. Then we see Hazel Brooks's legs insinuating themselves towards the camera as Garfield pounds the heavy bag, and we know these gams are attached to a dame who's got to be nothing but trouble. Garfield even fails to visit his mother as he descends, and the tune "Body and Soul" plays in the background. He gets the big fight and plans to go into the tank in exchange for the dough; there is the great shadowy shot of Garfield in a room with a dozen gangsters working out the deal. But then it turns out the whole neighbourhood is pulling for their corner boy. The kid from the delicatessen reminds Garfield of what certain people are doing over in Europe "to people like us just because of our religion." If that's not enough to convince him, Garfield's trainer, the great Canada Lee, dies on the eve of the fight. We know, before Garfield does, that he's not going to throw the fight. And a magnificent fight it is, filmed by Jimmy Howe on roller skates. In the last round, Garfield knocks his man out. He is redeemed and now deserves Lilli Palmer. (Since this is cinema, not real life, Garfield's honourable act will presumably put him beyond the reach of mobsters angry about being double-crossed.)

No sooner was the movie released in 1947 than Rossen, Garfield and scriptwriter Abraham Polonsky were dragged into House Committee on Un-American Activities hearings. In the twisted minds of these guardians of the public good, Garfield, Rossen and Polonsky were Jewish artists raising the "Jewish Question," which the committee equated with anti-Americanism. Furthermore, the gangsters in *Body and Soul* were presumed to be symbols of evil capitalism, the copout ending notwithstanding.

Ironically, *Body and Soul*, which rescued United Artists from the brink of bankruptcy, had started out to be a movie called *Tiger, Tiger Burning Bright*, based on the life of three-time welterweight champion and war hero Barney Ross. The theme was to have been basically the same. But before filming could begin, Ross announced he was a drug addict. He had gotten hooked on heroin and morphine in an army hospital following his heroics on Guadalcanal. That killed *Tiger, Tiger Burning Bright*. After all, not even a compromise ending was going to redeem an anticapitalist movie where the hero was a Jewish junkie. Ross's story was filmed by the same studio in more liberal times as *Monkey on My Back* (1957).

There is nothing symbolic about *The Set Up*. It is a cinematic exploration of human dignity and the horrible banality of evil. The movie lasts seventy-two minutes and covers the same period of time in the life of an aging heavyweight named Stoker Thompson (Robert Ryan). Stoker can't even claim has-been status because he was never anything more than a small-time palooka. Having lost his last four matches, he is reduced to fighting in the bout that follows the main event. He awaits his fate in a crummy hotel room across the street from the arena. His wife has left him because she can't stand to see him take another beating, and his manager has such a low opinion of Stoker's abilities that he gratefully accepts a measly half a yard to sell him out. Because he doesn't want to split the fifty and because he assumes Stoker will lose anyway, George Tobias, usually a comic figure but here cast against type, doesn't bother telling his fighter about the arrangement.

Who can forget Ryan's heartbreaking nighttime walk from the hotel to the arena? Or the shot of him sitting alone in the dressing room, surrounded by young hopefuls too dumb to see in him their own possible futures. Or the punch-drunk palooka selling programs, the blind ex-fighter listening to the punches, the fans spitting at the losers. In against an up-and-coming youngster, Stoker turns in the fight of his life. Ryan does a credible job in the fight scenes, grimly staged by director Robert Wise. At the film's end, Stoker leaves the dressing room to wait alone in the runway for the gangsters to come and settle with him.

Wise should have known he couldn't do a better boxing movie than *The Set Up*, but he tried in 1955, the result being a paean to middle-class values: *Somebody Up There Likes Me*. The only decent things about this bio of forties middleweight champ Rocky Graziano are the East Side street scenes and the fact that Paul Newman got the part rather than MGM's original choice, James Dean. The film is not exactly filled with dramatic tension, since we know Rocky's going to turn out all right and be called "goombah" on television by Martha Raye. Newman is dynamic and roguishly engaging, but he can't fight a lick.

There was another boxing movie that same year. If *Somebody* preached, "I can," *The Harder They Fall* was sheer cant. It is about a circus strongman named Toro (Mike Lane), who is absolutely lacking in boxing ability or any athletic coordination but is guided to a heavyweight championship bout by a crooked fight manager called Benko (Rod Steiger). After the title fight, in which Toro is nearly killed by the champ—former real-life champ Max Baer (who actually did kill two men in the ring)—reporter Humphrey Bogart begins his news story, and ends the movie, with the line, "Professional boxing should be banned even if it takes an act of Congress to do it." The main problem with this "exposé" is that everyone in the sport is bad, everyone opposed to it good. The sanctimonious Bogart takes it upon himself to tell Toro before the big fight that the strongman's whole career has been a fraud. And the movie is full of holes. How could somebody convince twenty-eight fighters, one after another, to go in the tank, and how come fans don't get wise? We're also supposed to believe a manager would only give a heavyweight challenger forty-nine dollars and seven cents after a championship fight.

Something must be said about *Raging Bull*. It is a well-acted character study with accurate scenes of Italian life as lived in the big cities of America. But a boxing movie it ain't, the fight scenes being the most pretentious ever filmed. As for Jake LaMotta, he would have been a creep no matter what his occupation. The same is true of Kirk Douglas's Midge Kelly character in *Champion*, 1949. Middleweight champ Kelly would just as certainly have alienated all those around him should he have chosen baseball or the stock market. The difference between these films is that *Champion* portrays boxing realistically, especially the particular relations between fighter and manager.

My own favourite boxing movie has to be King Vidor's 1931 giant, *The Champ*, starring Wallace Beery and Jackie Cooper. Beery, an ex-pug, is living above a gym in Tijuana with his little boy, Jackie Cooper. His wife, Irene Rich, left him years earlier. Beery by now has run to fat; he likes his booze and the racetrack, and his son adores him. Suddenly Irene Rich appears out of the past to rescue the kid from this tawdry world. Through an alcoholic haze, Beery decides to prove himself worthy of his son's love and admiration, and he gets on the comeback trail. But it is not easy; otherwise, we would not have the great Dickensian scene where the champ is trying to sleep one off while the kid urges him to start his workout in the seediest fight club ever committed to celluloid. "C'mon, Champ, you gotta get up!"

"Aww," growls Beery, turning over on the squeaky cot, "I don't wanna go to work." But he does. He fights the Mexican and wins, only to die in the dressing room in the little boy's arms.

So which actor displayed the best boxing skills? There are few indeed to attain realism's rankings, and this is what we discussed on the set of *Rocky IV* at the Agrodome in Vancouver, Sylvester Stallone and myself. How would his alter ego, Rocky Balboa, have made out in the ring against cinematic fighters of the past?

Rocky Balboa would have made a veritable bum-of-the-month club, we agreed, out of the likes of Kirk Douglas, Paul Newman and Stallone's particular nemesis, Ryan O'Neal in *Main Event*. (Actually, O'Neal has the better skills, but who was I to argue?) A little tougher would have been the two Galahads: Wayne Morris, who played more boxers than any other actor, and Elvis Presley. The latter, although soft and flabby—looking, according to one critic, like a pudgy Linda Darnell—did have some moves that might have been worked on by his trainer Charles Bronson. Robert Ryan was an old-fashioned stand-up fighter, courageous but easy to hit for a guy like Balboa. TKO in the fifth. Cagney in any of his pictures would have made for an interesting fight. Cagney could really dance and throw combinations but Rocky, according to his creator, would have eventually landed the big bomb somewhere around the ninth round.

Balboa's toughest opponent, the star declared, would have been James J. Corbett as played by Errol Flynn in *Gentleman Jim*. Flynn had style and grace, liked to show off but at any moment was liable to forget he was a gentleman and unleash that fury. Stallone magnanimously admitted that Balboa might even have needed to go the distance with Flynn. The Philly pug would, of course, have taken a unanimous decision. "So that leaves Rocky Balboa, the undisputed champion of the world," Stallone concluded.

"You're forgetting somebody," I said. "Chaney in *Hard Times*, Charles Bronson."

"He looks good but Balboa's too powerful for him. His style's made for Rocky. It would be like Hagler-Hearns, Foreman-Frazier. Balboa kayo in the fourth."

Perhaps I was too quick in saying, "No way." Perhaps I could have been more diplomatic in advancing my own opinion, which was, essentially, that Balboa would have had to take five punches to try and land one, but when he tried, Chaney wouldn't be there. It might have gone eight rounds but Chaney would have cut him up bad and taken the technical knockout.

Bronson moves with a grace and fluidity that not only had never been seen in boxing films but has rarely been equalled in the ring itself; Billy Conn, Tommy Loughran and Jersey Joe Walcott moved like that. As an authentic display it is unmatched, and Bronson's performance is made all the more remarkable by the fact that the actor was fifty-four years old when the film was made in 1975.

Stallone looked at me like I was a cretin and a traitor. "Rocky'd kill him."

In his eyes I glimpsed the brief moment when reel life and real life converged. He gave me a touch of the old streets-of-Philadelphia glare, then got up and walked away in his red, white and blue trunks.

Bad Week

November 5–12, 1988

The audience is screaming, stomping its feet and slamming beer bottles on tabletops. Not unusual behaviour in Vancouver's Commodore Ballroom, a place that usually offers up rock bands, but tonight this raucous conduct is prompted by the closed-circuit screen going blank just as the bell rings for the first round of the Matthew Hilton-Robert "Bam Bam" Hines fight.

Between this Friday and next, Canadian boxers will have

three world-title fight opportunities. Probably at no other time have two Canadians held world championships, as do Hilton (junior middleweight) and Donny Lalonde (light heavyweight). Of course, these titles are somewhat debased given the proliferation of sanctioning bodies. Next Friday, Willie Featherstone challenges Virgil Hill for the WBA light heavyweight title, thus raising the possibility of there being three Canadian world champs, two in the same division.

Matthew is certainly the most exciting fighter of the three. He has two brothers, Alex and Davey Junior, who are also boxers. They are true pugilistic progeny; their grandfather was a prize fighter as was their father, Dave Senior, who, if this were his era, would no doubt be a world champion. He was the kind of guy who took on any opponent, anywhere, at any weight from welter to light heavy. He was known to take a drink at the places where he fought and at places in between. He is famous for packing his young family into the car and driving from contest to contest. He fought and drank, fought and drank. A couple of his sons are known to have a fondness for alcohol, and not all of their fights have been within ropes and governed by rules. Indeed, trouble has been the Hiltons's most formidable opponent; they've confronted it many more times than Willie Pep fought Sandy Sadler or Rocky Graziano, Tony Zale. Montreal papers seem to have a standard set of heads devoted to the family: "Alex Hilton Vows He'll Stop Being Wild . . . Davey Ready To Put Past Behind Him . . . Dave Hilton on the Wagon." Only Matthew—"the clean-living Hilton"—seems to have been spared a bad press. While he has been preparing for the fight with Hines, his brother Alex is standing trial on charges of assault, sexual assault and forcible confinement stemming from incidents at Quebec's Bordeaux Prison where he is incarcerated.

A few years back, the Hiltons signed a promotional contract with Don King, who promised them many big fights and many millions of dollars. Matthew did get the opportunity to fight, and beat, Buster Drayton for the junior middleweight crown in 1987, but has been virtually inactive since then. He became disenchanted and ballooned to 194 pounds. "Maybe I was too young to understand," he told a reporter, "but when I won the title I thought that was all there was to it, being a champion fighter. I didn't have any idea about all the leeches and politics and deals that went along with it. I didn't even care about the money when I fought Drayton, I just wanted to be the champion." Over the objections of his father, Matthew jumped to promoter Bob Arum who, he says, has got him back on the road to where he wants to go, "and plowed it very nicely."

Matthew has choir-boy looks and an engaging child-like voice. He is certainly the most popular of the three Canadians featured this week. With the folks at the Commodore, Hilton is even more of an attraction than the hard-core fan's perennial favourite Thomas "Hit Man" Hearns, who tonight is up against James "the Heat" Kinchen. Also on the card are the middleweight of the future, Michael Nunn, and the aging Argentine Juan Roldan. None of these fighters have "transcended" their sport, becoming media darlings because they are palatable to the public. Therefore, at the Commodore this evening there is a dearth of dilettantes. It is definitely a fight crowd.

Tables are lined up perpendicular to the two huge screens, and I sit at the front with my friend Joe Ferone and various acquaintances. As the bell rings to start the first fight, Hilton catapults from his stool and into darkness. For the next eight minutes, including the one-minute rest periods between rounds, there will only be scattered snapshots of action. Unfortunately, there is sound, and we can hear the ring announcers exclaiming, "Hilton has him in trouble! . . . Hines is back against the ropes!" Naturally this provokes the crowd to yell and scream. For the briefest instant, we see Hilton pummelling Hines. But the screen goes blank again, as the announcer shouts, "And Hines is down!" The Commodore begins to shake from the hollering and stomping of feet.

Hilton, we hear, puts Hines down again. Somebody in charge apologizes over the public address system for "technical difficulties beyond our control." And promises, "We will soon have a visual." We do. The third round begins with a picture. There is an intake of breath, then, after several moments, a collective sigh of relief as it seems that the picture will probably remain. But there will be no exaltation tonight. No more knockdowns of Mr. Hines. Hardly a left hand from Mr. Hilton. After the fourth round, the momentum of the fight changes. The announcers are now in agreement that Hines is a legitimate "Philadelphia fighter," the kind of boxer who comes to fight and does not give up. And any fighter is encouraged upon realizing that his opponent is not utilizing his best weapon. Hines, as a southpaw, shoots out that right-hand jab and there is no responding left hook.

And so it goes until the end. There is no doubt about the outcome; Hines is the winner and new champion. In the postfight interview, Hines says, "I'm happy to be able to prove I'm the champion of Philadelphia." When one announcer calls attention to Hines's slip of the tongue, the other one says, "Maybe it amounts to the same thing."

Between rounds of the next bout, Hilton, wearing a sport shirt and shades, tells the announcers that he had torn cartilage on his left side just a few days earlier, that he should have called off the fight but didn't want to be known as a quitter. Every left hand thrown was agony. "But I don't want to make excuses."

In the second fight, Michael Nunn, a middleweight often compared to Sugar Ray Leonard but more reminiscent of a young, coltish Muhammad Ali, toys with Roldan, the aging and out-of-shape Argentinian. The older boxer's routine is pure macho, not so much his fighting as his adherence to the Argentine custom of never sitting down between rounds, no matter how tired he is, no matter how badly beaten. And at the end he is both.

Some wit once opined that the Tommy Hearns of recent outings "should build a glass house to hold his glass jaw." The validity of this crack is evidenced early on in the third bout, when James Kinchen, a fighter Hearns would have demolished a few years ago, decks him with one shot. Hearns staggers to his feet, grabs Kinchen and holds on for dear life—and dear career. He manages to last out the fight and even get a split decision, despite being knocked down and having a point taken away for holding. In an interview after the fight, an exasperated Kinchen divests himself of a deep sigh, saying, "Christmas this year came early for Tommy."

Saturday, November 5, two days before Donny Lalonde is to meet Sugar Ray Leonard in Las Vegas in defence of his WBC light heavyweight championship. Also there for the taking is the newly devised, mostly bogus and emotionally irrelevant super middleweight championship. With a limit of 168 pounds, the super middleweight is just another video division, television's theory being that more divisions mean more champions, and more championship fights mean more viewers.

I've had the strangest idea in my head today: that Lalonde is going to win. Sure, the odds are three-and-a-half to one against that happening, but so what? Lalonde is in against an older, smaller man who has not fought for two years, and has only fought twice in six years. Leonard has to be rusty. In his first comeback attempt after surgery to repair a detached retina, Leonard was knocked down by a club fighter named Kevin Howard. Now the former champion is six years older, and Lalonde hits harder than Howard. I have a feeling that Leonard will make Donny look foolish for four or five rounds, then he'll get hit by a big right hand from Lalonde and it will be all over. Although I have known it would happen since late June when Lalonde dropped a hint over lunch in Winnipeg, it is only now that this fight has begun to really interest me. There is the excitement and expectancy, "the obsessive appeal," in Joyce Carol Oates's words, of "an emotional experience impossible to convey in words."

Innumerable boxing people, as well as fans, have tried to convey this particular and peculiar emotional experience in words, as have the sport's detractors. But nothing I've heard, or read, has succeeded in capturing the feeling. I recall the doctor in Trinidad, questioning his response to the imminent Lalonde-Stewart fight: "Why do I feel this way? Me, a middle-aged adult? I don't even know anything about boxing. I don't have a favourite, really. But I feel like I'm six years old and about to walk downstairs on Christmas morning." The doc then turned to the oldest guy in the crowd, a veteran of the fight scene, a guy who promoted a few of Ali's fights in the seventies, and asked, "How come I feel this way?"

"That's boxing, man. Now you got it."

Joe Ferone telephones to ask if I've been able to get any money down on Lalonde. He knows I've been thinking along the lines of a ninth-round knockout, and suggests I could probably get ten to one on a Lalonde kayo inside that time. He also favours the Golden Boy and figures he can pick up some action at the Commodore. We discuss the possibilities, and he remarks that I don't sound so sure now. I'm not; in my morning paper I came across a morsel that had a distinctly upsetting taste. It seems Lalonde has been meditating with Mike Love of the Beach Boys, and Love has presented the fighter with a "meditation table." Lalonde's otherwise astute management has no business letting a person like Love enter Donny's orbit within a week of a fight. Lalonde is always in superb condition, but boxing is primarily mental. A fighter goes into the ring, particularly a major contest, in a very delicate mental state. His perspective has to be *managed*. He has to be in the proper mood, and this mood has nothing to do with anything that has anything to do with the Beach Boys. Would that Teddy Atlas—the young trainer with the old-guard philosophy fired early on by Lalonde's management—had been around to throw the guy out.

Monday evening is fight night. We're back at the Commodore, where Joe has saved us seats at the front. His friend Jeff is there along with a few ring rats like trainer Merv Seely and Dave Cooke. Joe goes off to hustle some bets but I stay where I am, growing more uncertain.

The undercard bouts are done. The fighters move to the ring. It is hard to read Lalonde's expression but he does not seem to be as self-contained as when he peered at Leslie Stewart across the ring in Trinidad. There are the shots of ringside celebrities: Bo Derek, David Brenner. Little interviews with Sylvester Stallone and Gene Hackman. Mike Tyson is there looking like a squat block of granite. The man makes the announcements and Canadians have to suffer the indignity of trumpeter Chuck Mangione playing "O Canada." Then the Pointer Sisters do "The Star-Spangled Banner." Waiting for the bell to begin round one, the Commodore is a nervous ballroom. The atmosphere fairly crackles.

There's the bell. They move together and Donny connects first, with a left jab, of all things. Leonard is not proceeding as expected. There is no dancing, no sticking and not much moving. Then—bam! Lalonde scores with a right and the place gets wild. But Leonard is still standing and Lalonde does not follow up. The first is obviously Donny's round, however. The second is more of the same. Lalonde lands more punches, but he also throws more. He misses too often, and looks awkward throwing right hands from too far away. He doesn't pull back on them even when he must know they are not going to land. The punches fall short, at the level of Leonard's solar plexus, leaving Donny open for left hooks.

The third round is better for Lalonde, and then in the fourth there's the hard right and Leonard goes down. When he comes up there is an obvious cut on the bridge of his nose. Now's the time, but Lalonde does not stay on him. The no-nonsense

Leonard makes his appearance in the fifth. He pops in those jabs for which he is famous, and takes advantage of Lalonde's feeble left hand and off-balance right. In the corner before the sixth, you can hear Ralph Citro hollering over the voice of Tommy Gallagher, "You got to get in two, three shots, son. Not just one. One's not going to take this man out."

He doesn't get them in during the sixth or the seventh, but Donny has a better round in the eighth. Then in the ninth it appears that he has Leonard. He gets the older boxer in a corner, scores a right, then another, but suddenly, as if he has just come awake, Leonard unleashes a furious barrage of lefts and rights and it is Lalonde who ends up on the canvas. He is up at eight but Leonard is there on top of him to finish the business. Lalonde is utterly defenceless, reacting to punches like an average guy, not like a prize fighter. He does not cover up instinctually. He looks like a man who realizes he is about to fall from a very high perch and is frantically groping for something—anything—to save himself. But there is no saving Lalonde, and down he goes again from extraordinary combinations. And that's it.

Lalonde is out cold. There is a terrible close-up of him lying unconscious, blood running from the corner of his right eye. While Donny's seconds and a doctor bend solemnly to administer to him, the camera pulls back to show Sugar Ray Leonard cantering about the ring while people try to embrace him. There is a long minute of fear. The crowd at the Commodore remains absolutely silent. Then it cheers as Lalonde finally stirs and is helped back to the stool in his corner.

There is a certain kind of person who derives enjoyment from making fun of the way fighters speak. I recall, as a kid, seeing a comedian at a mob-inspired nightclub doing his impersonation of Joe Louis at a postfight interview. I was only ten or eleven at the time, so I must have been taken to the club by my father to watch the fights that were on before the stage show. It was the Marciano era, the place was called Palumbo's, and the guy's mouth was hanging open dumbly as he muttered, "It was . . . uh . . . tough fight . . . but ah . . . knowed ahd git da man . . . soonah . . . or . . . layah." In the white version, the fighter is strictly a dese-dem-and-dose, cauliflower-ear, bent-nose kind of guy, a palooka. "So, yeah, I hit da bum and den I hit em anudder time, an den he don't get up no more. I wanna say hello da my mudder . . ."

Personally, I find the interviews that take place immediately after a fight to be simply astonishing. The fighter has undergone physical and emotional trauma of a kind that few people can empathize with or even comprehend. He has possibly seen his entire life and career turned around. Given all this, it is amazing that the guy can manage to say anything at all coherent. Yet there was James Kinchen having just battled Tommy Hearns, knowing he had really beaten the man, facing the unreality of the decision—the robbery was worth at least a million dollars—but having the grace and dignity to crack a resigned joke about Christmas coming early for Tommy. Matthew Hilton, going into the ring with an injury and the immense burden of being a Hilton, losing the fight and his championship, knowing he had to begin an even bigger battle to re-establish himself, and speaking in his little kid's voice about not wanting to make excuses. Robert Hines, rejoicing that he was now champion of Philadelphia, despite his awkwardness being not a wit less articulate than Michael Nunn, who was glib, cocky, jiving and basking in the glow of his prospects and the comfortable embrace of the cameras.

But I've never seen a postfight interview more revealing or touching than Donny Lalonde's following his bout with Leonard. Here was a young man who had just been knocked unconscious for a full minute by a man considered one of the greatest fighters of all time. Lalonde had been this close to pulling off one of the biggest upsets in boxing history. Now he couldn't even stand on his own—he was supported during the interview by David Wolf and Tommy Gallagher—yet had to reply to the inane question, "Tell us, Donny, how do you feel?" Lalonde started to answer, shook his head, and spoke to himself out loud, "I can't believe this has happened." It was then, for the first time, that I liked the man. He refused to be confined and diminished by the frame of a television screen. Beat-up and utterly exhausted, he nevertheless displayed great courage under unimaginable duress; in perfect response to everything that had transpired and that which would *not* now transpire, he then uttered a consummate, "Shit!"

Willie Featherstone and Virgil Hill will step into the ring in Bismarck, North Dakota, on Friday, which just happens to be exactly 167 years to the day since the pugilistic encounter of Bill Neate and Tom Hickman (also known as the Gasman, or just plain Gas) at Hungerford, Berkshire, England. So far as I know, the coincidence of a championship fight occurring on the anniversary of this historic occasion has been marked by no one. That long-ago engagement was the subject of an 1821 essay by William Hazlitt called "The Fight." The assistant editor of *New Monthly Magazine* wished to reject the piece on the basis of its "vulgarity" but the editor prevailed, calling the essay "a picture of manners . . . a history painting." Hazlitt turned in four thousand words, about three hundred of them devoted to the actual bout.

Although prize fighting was immensely popular in England in Hazlitt's day, it was also of questionable legality. The location of a bout was a well-kept secret, known only to "the Fancy," the fight crowd, as insurance against the intrusion of the constabulary acting at the behest of nettlesome do-gooders. Hazlitt was not quite part of the Fancy, though he was an ardent enthusiast of the milling game, as he was of many other things. He didn't know where the fight would be held until the very eve of the bout, when he finally got the dope at a London pub called the Hole in the Wall. Then there remained the matter of finding a coach that would get him to Hungerford in time. This he did and, upon reaching his destination, passed a sleepless but enjoyable night bending his elbow and engaging in fight talk at the Crown Inn.

I know where *my* fight is to take place, although getting there is, in this age of jet travel, no easy matter, let alone finding any of the Fancy to talk boxing with along the way. My first conversation about the match takes place at U.S. Customs, Vancouver airport.

Officer Garrett: Why are you going to Bismarck?

JC: A prize fight. (*Half a minute passes with no response.*) A boxing match.

Garrett: I *know* what a prize fight is. But I didn't know they even had a *ring* in Bismarck. Are you in it?

JC: Are you kidding?

Garrett: What fight is it?

JC: WBA light heavyweight championship.

Garrett: Who's the champ?

JC: Virgil Hill.

Garrett: Never heard of him.

JC: You're not the only one.

Garrett: What's your reason for going?

JC: I'm a writer.

Garrett: Are you in the association?

JC: What association is that, sir?

Garrett: Uh, well, the writers' association?

This question gives me pause, but I have to admit that I am not. The answer seems to please him—as does the truth of it please me—and Officer Garrett bids me pass.

In the lounge at the departure gate I read a press account of Bill Ballenger, Donny Lalonde's friend and business partner, watching the Lalonde-Leonard fight at their Corner Boy's Tavern and weeping copious tears. Later, during a three-hour stopover in Denver, I pass some time in a cafe-bar. It is voting day, but no one seems to give a damn about who will be their next president. The latest Broncos game dominates discussions and newspaper space. Neither the *Post* nor the *Rocky Mountain News* carry anything about the previous night's fight.

At the tiny Bismarck airport I pick a motel from the advertising board and the manager comes out to get me. The Fleck House Best Western is located downtown and I have a pleasant, old-fashioned vision of city centre and all that entails. I don't know where fight headquarters is but assume it will be in town. The motel manager is a bearish fellow who doesn't know much about boxing and is actually against the city holding prize fights. "Don't make the town enough money, too much trouble." He doesn't know about a press rate, either. "Coupla fellas from AP out of Fargo stop by a few times a year and I give 'em my salesman's discount. Two dollars off."

Eleven o'clock at night and all is dark and quiet except to the northeast, where there is the familiar glow of a 7-Eleven. When I open the door, the clerk looks up from his girlie magazine and sidles over to the cash register. His hand seeks the drawer below. I smile at him. Back in the U.S. of A. Instead of pulling a gun, I buy a club soda and the local paper. "Knockout Predicted," it reads over the by-line of the sports editor. "Featherstone Says Hill Won't Go Distance."

Next morning I step out onto the deserted streets of downtown. No rushing, distracted businesspeople, no secretaries clicking by on errands, no corn-fed, plains-bred entrepreneurs with cellular phones glued to their ears driving cowboy Cadillacs. Not even one farmer come into town for a coffee. It is like the small-city set at some all-American theme park during the off-season. It takes me twenty minutes to find a place to have breakfast. The other customers observe me carefully: the stranger. I order hot cakes, and mind my own business and my newspaper.

Virgil Hill and Willie Featherstone seem to have only their obscurity in common. Featherstone doesn't possess an Olympic medal. He doesn't spring from a fighting family or dye his hair blond and espouse new age ideas. He is, however, the light heavyweight champion of the entire British Commonwealth as well as of Canada. This fact translates into the occasional line in the newspapers in his hometown, Toronto. Nothing more. Hill is one of the highly touted crop of boxing medallists from the 1984 Olympics, light heavyweight champion of the WBA share of the world, and an extremely handsome fellow into the bargain. Yet he is virtually unknown outside of North Dakota, which he calls his home state and which claims him despite his being born in Missouri and residing in Las Vegas.

That year's Olympic medal winners had their coming-out party at Madison Square Garden on November 15, 1984. Mark Beland, Tyrell Biggs, Evander Holyfield, Pernell Whitaker and Meldrick Taylor all got to fight on ABC prime time. But Hill's fight, in which he knocked out one Arthur Wright in two, was the opening act, happening before the cameras started to roll. So his professional career began with a snub, and was followed by three years of disregard. He became the misplaced Olympian. Rather than fighting in New York, Vegas and Atlantic City like his peers, Hill was slotted into places like Everett, Washington, and Lancaster, Pennsylvania. He secured the allegiance of his home state by battling in Bismarck, Williston, Grand Forks and Fargo. Even though he scored plenty of knockouts, he was dismissed as a powder-puff puncher until May 1, 1987, when he knocked out former cruiserweight champion Marvin Camel in the first round in Fargo. Then, fighting every six weeks, Hill knocked out tough Marcos Geraldo in two, decisioned Junior Edmond, kayoed Leslie Stewart for the WBA title and defended with a twelve-round decision over Rufino Angulo in Paris.

After breakfast I set out for fight headquarters. Although Bismarck is the capital of North Dakota, it has no public transportation. It does have a cab company, but on this particular morning the company's phone line is down. Cabs don't cruise the streets looking for fares because there are no people on the streets. Except for me. I am forced to hike the mile and a half to fight central at the Holiday Inn. Once there I immediately run into Joey Edwards, a trainer and member of the boxing and black communities of Edmonton. A little guy with grey hair curling up from under his cap, Joey is working with Danny Stonewalker, who is scheduled to fight Joe Lasisi, ranked in the world's top ten by every organization, in the semi-main event. We fall to discussing mutual Edmonton friends, the bluesman Big Miller and the late, lamented Nick Zubray, mayor of Tap City.

Freddy Roach, the recently retired welterweight, comes down for a late breakfast, accompanied by none other than the grand old man Eddie Futch. Small and natty, Futch goes back to the early Joe Louis era. He has trained Archie Moore, George Foreman, Joe Frazier, Michael Spinks and dozens of others. I pass along greetings from Vancouver welterweight Jamey Ollenberger, who had gone to California a couple of years earlier to study under Futch. "Oh, what a nice kid Jamey is," he says. I tell him that Jamey had mangled his foot in a motorcycle accident and will never fight again. This leads Futch to discourse on all the fighters he's known who have been killed or injured on motorcycles. "The two don't go together. There was Young Stribling . . ."

"You knew him?"

"Yes, I did. And it was right after his fight with Jack Dempsey that he was back home in Georgia riding on a motorcycle. A car passed too close and tore his foot off. He died. And James Schuler . . ."

Schuler was a middleweight from Philadelphia who'd been on the Spinks card in Vancouver in November of '83. He was a sweet kid. With the winnings from his subsequent loss to Thomas Hearns, he went back to Philadelphia, bought a motorcycle and was killed in an accident the same day. Schuler reminds Futch of another tragedy that claimed one of his own fighters just three months earlier. "This boy was a nice kid, a welterweight with real promise. He could move and hit with either hand. He was 7 and 0 while still in school. Then he went to his high-school graduation party at a lake in Nevada. The kids all swam out towards a platform floating in the middle of the lake. The other kids got there and looked around but the boy wasn't with them, and he wasn't swimming. He just drowned and nobody heard him or saw him."

Futch folds his hands on the table and stares at them. The skin is loose on his long fingers. He looks up and smiles rather shyly, as if he is worried about casting a pall over the gathering. He changes the topic, turning to me. "Now you mentioned Joe Frazier earlier. It's a funny thing, I had a *feeling* about him right away. I was out in California and got a call from his people in Philadelphia. Some businessmen had gotten together to back him. They wanted me to have a look. I didn't know anything about him, really, other than that he had won the gold medal in the Olympics. They told me he had a professional record of 7 and 0 but I'd never seen him fight. Well, they came out. I met them at the airport. Yancey Durham brought him. They came up to me in the airport and right away it happened. I didn't have to see Frazier in the gym. There was a connection. I knew it would be all right."

Eddie Futch is an articulate speaker who doesn't waste words. Somewhere between his carefully engineered speech and the crude bombast of most other trainers and managers stands and enunciates Ray Rutter of Oakville, Ontario, manager of Willie Featherstone and several other fighters. For a couple of years he published his *Ray Rutter's Boxing News*, a monthly compendium of information and controversy that owed much to the Flash Gordon school of journalism. Gordon was a New York fight fanatic, now in exile, who haunted the gyms, the arenas and the microfilm readers, digging up the story behind the story, the dirt. But Ray has never been an imitator. The opinions he dispensed were his own, and he backed them up with information. Without his sadly missed monthly missal to speak for him, he has had to hone his elocutionary skills. He advocates and declaims with the slightest encouragement but always make the words jump. As for the chips, he lets them fall where they may. Rutter has an unimpeachable reputation for integrity, which is a good thing, because he can also, when in the mood, charm the birds right out of the trees. I know because he later charmed the entire town of Bismarck.

This fight marks the first time Featherstone has fought outside of Canada in his entire career. Yet in the past year, with a match in Halifax and one in Toronto, the fighter made $50,000, which is mostly a testament to Rutter's negotiating skills. In addition, Featherstone operates his own appliance repair business in Scarborough, netting him an additional forty thousand a year. Soft-spoken, ruggedly handsome and sort of shy, Willie is also happily married with a brand-new daughter.

Featherstone has his final workout that afternoon at a community centre outside of town. I get a ride with Mort Sharnik, publicist for the promoters, Ringside International Boxing Incorporated. A big, heavy-set, white-haired boxing veteran, Sharnik got his start as a writer for *Sports Illustrated*. During the drive, he asks me what is going on in Vancouver, and I have to tell him there hasn't been a card in two years.

Featherstone and Stonewalker are shadowboxing in a ring set up beyond a row of basketball bleachers. I am immediately surprised at how much bigger Featherstone has gotten since the last time I saw him. He was always just a little too heavy for a middleweight, yet not quite a full-fledged light heavy. Lifting weights has thickened his arms and shoulders. He moves about the ring throwing punches, bobbing and weaving. His trainer, and father, Terry, keeps time. Three minutes of moving, a minute of rest.

Although Stonewalker and Featherstone share the ring, the two men never look at each other and never get in each other's way, as if their moves have been choreographed. Stonewalker, known until recently as Danny Lindstrom, is taller and brokennosed. Although solidly built and in condition, he displays the smooth skin and lack of muscular definition that seem to be an Indian trait. Both men have trained for the past month at the Hobbema Reserve in Alberta. The reserve is the richest in Canada, yet oil money has not meant an end to social problems. The Hobbema elders had the idea of beginning a serious boxing program and got hold of trainer and ex-fighter Jim Gillio of Brooklyn, New York, to be the organizer and consultant.

Featherstone had a brilliant amateur career, winning eighty-four times while losing only seven bouts, and becoming North American amateur middleweight champion. He turned pro on January 17, 1978, in Toronto with a third-round knockout of future world super middleweight champion Murray Sutherland. By January 1982, his pro record was 9 and 2, the losses generally conceded to be the result of hometown decisions in Montreal and Winnipeg. But it was that month that Featherstone became another name on Eddie Futch's motorcycle victim list.

When they lifted the bike off the fighter, they found him covered in his own blood, with two broken kneecaps and a cracked vertebra. The doctors maintained he would be crippled for life; the newspapers declared, "Promising Boxing Career Ended." But Featherstone was having no part of these predictions. Somehow, in the midst of his nightmare, he summoned the resolve to walk again. With that first awkward step, he became determined he would not go hobbling through life. Later, he found the courage to push himself through a punishing program of conditioning, his new goal being to fight again. On June 22, 1984, Featherstone won an eight-round decision over Tony Corovic in Toronto. It might have seemed like a decidedly unspectacular performance to the casual observer, but it was a miraculous achievement to those who knew Featherstone's story.

Willie devoted the next six months to improving his conditioning and working on skills he had heretofore ignored, mainly defensive ones. He had always been a follower of the best-defence-is-a-good-offence philosophy of pugilism. Terry Featherstone endeavoured to make his boy an all-round fighter, but his son's second comeback bout did not provide the blackboard for a display of recent lessons. He knocked Bill Hollis out in the first round. Featherstone ran his comeback string to 6 and 0 before dropping a decision to Danny Stonewalker (then Lindstrom). Despite the loss, it was Willie and not Danny who got a shot two months later at Canadian light heavyweight champion Roddy McDonald. Donny Lalonde, Featherstone's nemesis and very much an unseen presence in Bismarck this week, had won the championship from McDonald three years earlier but lost it to the bureaucrats at the Canadian Boxing Federation. McDonald reclaimed the championship and, in turn, relinquished it to Willie, who also beat him in a rematch at the beginning of 1987. Featherstone then pulled off an upset victory, taking the Commonwealth crown from Zambia's Enoch Chama. Next he got his revenge on Lindstrom. Then in May 1988, he kayoed Dave Fiddler in Hawkesbury, Nova Scotia, in nine rounds. And now he was in Bismarck.

For Willie, the fight with Hill represents what sportswriters love to call "the crossroads." One way leads to the big time and big bucks, the other to the end of the line. Rutter says they have offers, win or lose. If it is lose, there is at least one more decent payday, the assurance of a Commonwealth defence in Australia. But there can't be much beyond that. Because of his injuries Featherstone is physically much older than thirty, and he is too smart to risk getting hurt for chump change in Canada.

One of the local sportswriters has called this "the week of coattails," Bush riding in on Reagan's, Hill and Featherstone catching a lift with Leonard-Lalonde. Mort Sharnik, hosting the prefight press conference, tries to shake off this line of thinking, assuring the crowd, "For the rest of the week Bismarck is the boxing capital of the world. The light heavyweights are hot!" The fighters, their managers and their trainers have a turn at the microphone, as do the promoter and the mayor, nicknamed the Hawk, who is quietly booed. An old Indian man presents Hill with a beautiful headdress.

Hill's own racial origins are a matter of controversy, at least in these parts. He looks like a light-skinned, fine-featured version of the actor Billy Dee Williams. He was adopted by white foster parents and is generally regarded in North Dakota as being part Indian. "It is much easier to be part Indian in North Dakota," a local newspaper editor assured me, "than to be part black." As Hill speaks, his wife-to-be, Denean Howard, a member of the silver-medal-winning 1600-metre relay team at the Seoul Olympics, beams at him while cradling their fourteen-month-old baby in her arms. Apart from a couple of fight guys, a couple of boxers and no more than three people in the stands on fight night, Ms. Howard is the only definitely black person to be seen in town all week. Not only is this the whitest fight scene I have ever witnessed, it is the whitest I can imagine.

Hill badmouths Donny Lalonde, and says he will knock Featherstone out. Willie badmouths Donny Lalonde, and says he will knock Hill out. Eddie Futch declares Hill ready to take his place in the line of great light heavyweights like Spinks, Moore, Ezzard Charles and John Henry Lewis. After Futch's historic references, Danny Stonewalker puts a funny coda on the proceedings: "I've had two good sleeps and I'm feeling like a grizzly bear, rarin' to go."

With nothing else to do the next afternoon, I hang around the motel room, watching a taped replay from Monaco of Monday afternoon's fight between the overrated Doug De Witt and the underrated Sumbu Kalambay. There is a terrible preliminary bout matching a Colombian and a Puerto Rican. The announcer sums it up well: "In the scheme of things this is the boxing equivalent of a bad lounge act." But Kalambay is superb, picture-book perfect. Moving fluidly, throwing rapier-like jabs, rights like range-finding missiles and left hooks in short explosive arcs. And he is in excellent condition, or, as the announcer observes, "in such good shape, he's not even breathing." He takes De Witt out with a left hook at 1:31 of the seventh round.

I flip off the TV, go to the window and pull back the heavy drapes. The view encompasses several blocks, yet the streets are deserted. Nothing moves except over at the 7-Eleven, where a car is pulling away from the gas pumps, its exhaust hanging like a white cloud on the cold, dry air. I flop on the bed, open my second cup of take-out coffee and begin to read. I have brought along a homemade anthology of chapters and sections photostatted from books, everything stapled together to make a highly irregular reading package for the trip.

As well as Hazlitt's report on the Neate-Hickman affair, I have Blaise Cendrars's memoir of the mysterious Arthur Cravan, nephew of Oscar Wilde, "poet with the world's shortest haircut" and one-time heavyweight boxing champion of Europe.

I also have the *J* section from the Penguin *Dictionary of Saints*, all the Joans, Johns and Josephs. I am proceeding in my search for the patron saint of prize fighters, obsessed by the vision of a reliquary glimpsed two years earlier while driving through an intersection on the outskirts of La Paz, Baja, California. The hood of an automobile was propped up on the ground, forming a cowl around a post on top of which sat a plaster saint. Below the saint—a woman—was nailed a poster that announced "BOXEO," and underneath were printed the bouts to be held three days hence in La Paz.

Thus I wile away the long Dakota afternoon. Finally, it is five o'clock and the bar at the Holiday Inn will be opening, so I call a taxi. After a while, I run into Eddie Futch. We talk about history's great light heavyweights. The greatest of these was Billy Conn, the 170-pound kid from Pittsburgh who had Joe Louis beaten and the heavyweight crown just three rounds from adorning his head when he got stupid and decided to slug. Up until that infamous twelfth round, Conn had turned in one of the most outstanding performances ever seen within the squared circle. "The next day," Futch said, "I bought several copies of each newspaper and took them back to my boxing club. I stuck the fight photographs up on the walls so they went all the way around the room. I said to the kids, '*This* is what boxing is supposed to be.' " The little man's eyes glowed with the memory of it.

Friday afternoon. Little to do now but mark the hours until fight time. I hike across the railroad tracks, where green Burlington Northern grain cars sit in the shadow of an old passenger station that has been converted into a dreary Mexican restaurant. A mile beyond the tracks is the Kirkwood Mall, which serves to answer my question about where all the people have gone. Acres of shops, acres of consumers. I have the same sense of dislocation you get on an airplane; the mall could be in Bismarck, Brisbane or Burnaby. Everyone looks basically the same, except for three guys. Two of them come into the drugstore where I am browsing at the magazine rack. I wonder about them until one picks up a boxing magazine. They are the WBA observers from Las Vegas. "Hey," one says to me. "You know Davey Pearl? He's out there." I look out to the mall and there is the diminutive referee, looking lost. We talk for a while, then go our separate ways.

As I arrive at the Civic Center that night, I think of Hazlitt's description of the site of the Hungerford bout: "The grass was wet, and the ground miry, and ploughed up with multitudinous feet . . ." The ground is miry here too, ploughed up by multitudinous bulldozers readying the spot for a layer of parking lot cement. In the pressroom perched in the rafters, a group of media types converges to inquire if I am the Canadian who penned the by-now-famous line, "Bismarck is the place where the hipsters from Minot go for a good time." Alas, I have to admit it was not I but one Steve Buffery of *The Toronto*

Sun. Down at ringside I encounter Davey Pearl. As the U.S. anthem is being sung, Davey stands at centre ring, hand over his heart, mouthing the words.

Stonewalker and Lasisi fight first. Stonewalker lands some shots and Lasisi's head moves jerkily to the left or right, like a toy mechanical soldier's. But when the black fighter scores, Stonewalker has more of a reaction. It takes the Canadian a fraction longer to refocus his attention. Still, the first is Danny's round. The second and third rounds might be scored for either man. Lasisi's bald head is knobby, his eyes hooded; he fights dirty. He holds Stonewalker behind the neck, hits him after the bell that ends the third.

During the fourth, I hear a guy in back of me ask his pal, "Where's the nigger from?"

"Nigeria," is the answer. "That's down by Louisiana."

Stonewalker takes the fourth; the fifth I score even. Then, in the sixth, Lasisi begins to get the left jab in. Towards the end of the round he opens a deep gash on Stonewalker's forehead and Davey Pearl separates the fighters. The referee examines the cut and waves his arms, stopping the fight. With only half a minute to go in the round, it seems a bit premature. Danny's shoulders sag with disappointment.

There is a terrible four-round fill-in fight. Then, five minutes later, a tremendous collective "BOOOOOO!" sounds, which means Willie Featherstone is approaching the ring. He climbs through the ropes and glides about the ring with wide sideways steps, looking at the canvas, head bent, the object of raucous disfavour. Earlier I had stopped in the dressing room to wish him luck. Seated on a bench surrounded by his people, Willie had nevertheless looked as alone as a man can be.

The boos trickle to scattered catcalls and then there is an explosion of enthusiasm as Hill, wearing the headdress and carrying his fourteen-month-old daughter, makes his way forward. He is preceded by a bodyguard, a biker type with a spur-of-the-moment haircut who holds the green championship belt aloft. Hill climbs into the ring. The noise ebbs as the headdress and robe are removed, but swells again as he begins to dance around the ring, "vigorous, elastic"; like Neate, he moves about "like a panther." I look around me and see no familiar facial types. This is not a fight crowd but a Virgil Hill crowd. The place is packed with young females. There are some older ones too, and even some preteens escorted by their parents. They all invoke Hill's name.

The secretary of the state of North Dakota is introduced, a short bulky fellow in a rumpled suit who conveys the governor's best wishes to Hill, who pays him absolutely no attention. There follows the ritual of the anthems, then a few overlong minutes as the ring is cleared of all but referee and combatants. "This is the trying time," wrote Hazlitt. "It is then the heart sickens, as you think what the two champions are about, and how short a time will determine their fate. . . . After the first blow is struck, there is no opportunity for nervous apprehensions; you are swallowed up in the immediate interest of the scene . . ."

There's the bell, a roar, and they move to meet each other. Willie throws a couple of right-hand leads. The first misses and brings no response but the next is greeted by a sharp left-right combination. A moment later, another missed right hand and sharp counterpunching by Hill. Only the blindest of Canadian nationalists could deny the superiority that Hill has so quickly evidenced, and that only the luckiest of wild punches will be able to refute. The first thirty seconds are an augury of the final outcome. Throughout the fight, after missing a punch or getting hit with one, Featherstone, keeping his distance, slams his gloves together and shouts. Later, Ray Rutter will say that Willie was just voicing his frustration at not being able to solve Hill's style.

In the third round, Hill puts Willie on the canvas for the first time in his career. And, as Hazlitt put it, "From this time forward the event became more certain every second. . . . My faintest hopes have faded from my sight."

After taking the mandatory eight count, Willie moves back into action as the crowd screams. I look behind me, up to where a "wave" is passing through the bleachers. I have never seen this at a boxing match. Most people are watching the progress of the wave rather than the fight. Hill clubs Featherstone behind the neck and Willie lands two rights at the end of the round. They are the best shots he will get in all evening.

Hill dominates the fourth round. Featherstone has his best time in the fifth, or, more accurately, it is Hill's worst. Willie lands a couple of right hands to which Hill responds by dropping his guard and taunting. This is an ugly piece of work, this bit of jive, but unfortunately it has become more and more prevalent since being introduced by Muhammad Ali. Hill will apologize for it later at the press conference. Two of the judges will score the fifth for Featherstone, the only round he will be credited with on any of the three scorecards.

Hill has a lacklustre sixth round, but Willie does nothing. The champion opens a cut over Featherstone's right eye in the seventh, scoring almost at will with the jab and straight right hand. Yet even as Hill rolls up the points, he reveals himself to be a mechanical fighter, doing everything well but without excitement. There is no superb artistry to revel in, as there is in watching Leonard. There is none of the dramatic expectancy you feel with Lalonde, knowing that at any time he may take his man out with one punch. In the tenth, a left hook sends Featherstone to the ropes, and the referee stops the fight. A TKO at two minutes and five seconds.

It is a very distraught young man who slumps on the bench in the dressing room minutes later. Featherstone has suffered a punctured eardrum, a cut below his right eye, cuts above and below his left eye, but he seems unmindful of his injuries. His torment, for the time being at least, is purely mental.

No sooner had I gotten back home than fight manager and agent Jimmy Johnston telephoned. While I was in North Dakota, J. J. had been in England with a heavyweight named Speed Christian. At the beginning of November, I had gone out to an arena in Burnaby with Johnston to meet his fighter, who hails from Jamaica via Halifax. Speed told me he'd had a "few" pro fights but his biggest claim to fame was going six rounds with Trevor Berbick in an exhibition.

"So we get to London," Jimmy Johnston is saying, "and when they see how good Speed looks, they substitute this guy named Big Bad James Oyebola, who is six-nine. He knocked Speed out in the first round and now they're trying to stiff us on the purse because they say he didn't get hit that hard. Well, I told them, that giant belted my guy all the way across the ring! Knocked out two of his teeth! Ah, man; it's bad news."

Yeah, a bad-news coda on a very bad week. In fact, for Canadian fighters, it has been the worst week there ever was.

Hustle, Scuffle and Ankle Express

Whenever I get discouraged about boxing, its venal corruption, the sorry manipulation of people and careers (as with Mike Tyson), the cheapening influence of television with its many divisions, I take courage from the stout hearts and overworked minds of those who down the decades have given the sport its colour. When thoroughly depressed, I lament the passing of so many characters, their places to remain unfilled forever. Those legends of bygone eras, like Doc Kearns and Philadelphia Jack

O'Brien, Good Time Charley Friedman and the boy bandit, Jimmy J. Johnston. Some of these rapscallions I have met personally, such as Cus D'Amato and Nick Zubray, the latter out of Edmonton, and known as the Mayor of Tap City after the tapped-out realm where he ruled.

But different versions of these people are still out there, like George Chuvalo and Tex Cobb, Bruce "the Mouse" Strauss and the guy who called me up at one the other morning to tell me about the guy who had called *him* at three in the morning. "Yeah, he calls from Yugoslavia, he's a matchmaker there. He wants to know if I can bring a good middleweight over. 'Sure,' I said, 'I got Gordy Lawson, he's 11 and 3.' Guy says, 'Great!' I ask him when's the fight; he says, 'Tomorrow.' Tomorrow! We were on a plane at four that afternoon. It took us twenty-two hours to get to Titograd. We rushed from the airport to the stadium, and there's 15,000 people in the stands waiting for us. Soon as I got Gordy's hands taped, they called us to the ring. The announcer must have told the crowd the story because we got a standing ovation from all 15,000 of them."

The speaker is Jimmy Johnston. Although he is fifty-nine years old and his grey hair is turning white, Johnston always seems to have the expression of a ten-year-old kid. Not the kind of ten-year-old who dutifully tends to his paper route and never misses a minute of Sunday school, however. No, it is the look of the kid who has just swiped his old man's credit card and is going to swing with a year's supply of chocolate.

Fifty-nine years old and he stills speaks with hushed glee of scams, hustles and adventure. You can't help but recall the words a New York judge spoke about the original Jimmy J. Johnston in the first decade of this century: "One sees the leer in his eye and fathoms that he has a rakish wit and must have his laugh." If James J. Johnston were not the name on his passport, you might think the guy had adopted it for purposes of homage or imitation. The careers of the two men follow a parallel course, but if the current J. J. does not appear as successful as the former, blame it on the seventy years between.

It should be noted that this J. J. shares wholeheartedly the belief of the former that "legitimate business is a figure of speech." And whereas the first boy bandit managed guys like Boer Rodel and Faintin' Phil Scott, the second brigand has had George Jerome and Scotty Walsh; fighters of similiar abilities, they too had their idiosyncrasies but no Runyon. The first J. J. managed Jack Johnson for one entire half-hour. The second managed Tommy Burns—*another* Tommy Burns—whose total career time in the ring didn't even add up to one entire half-hour. The first had a fake Boer War hero in his stable, but some people have been so unkind as to intimate that all of the second's fighters have been impostors. This is certainly not the case. It must be said, however, that a number of incidents in Jimmy Johnston's varied career in boxing have about them an aura of ambiguity.

He got the boxing bug early, fighting as an amateur, including three times in the Golden Gloves. Simultaneous with his early fistic forays, he was writing about the sport, selling his first piece to *Ring* magazine when he was fifteen years old. The Second World War interrupted his career. He joined the merchant marine and saw the world. He stayed on the boats after the conflict ended and saw the world a few more times. He also saw boxing matches wherever he went: Sydney, Suva or San José. When he got back to Vancouver in 1949, J. J. had a few more amateur fights, started his own amateur club and then turned pro. He had two pro fights, but "they were of no consequence," he says.

After an unfortunate misunderstanding about some diamonds, Johnston retired for a year to the crowbar hotel. Upon his return in the early fifties, he began booking fights and promoting shows in Burnaby, North Vancouver and outlying cities such as Creston, Nelson and Prince George. "In those days," he recalls wistfully, "you could go into a town and get an arena, and cooperation, for a hundred-dollar bill." In the sixties, he began publishing a magazine called *Fistic Flashes*, a monthly compendium of boxing news and opinions. Even now, in the unlikely event of there being a fight card in the Vancouver area, it is Johnston who produces the program.

As a manager, his biggest success was with George Jerome, who briefly held the Canadian heavyweight championship in the late seventies upon the retirement of George Chuvalo. "We didn't have *that* for long. I should have listened to old Nick Zubray. He was always right. We got the chance to fight Paul "the Investment" Nielsen in Toronto. Nick told me not to take the fight but I figured Jerome had beaten Horst Geisler and Geisler had beaten Nielsen, so I ignored his advice. Nielsen stopped Jerome in the eighth." As manager and booking agent, J. J. kept busy dispatching guys to fight throughout Canada and the United States. In this he was no different from a couple of dozen other North American boxing hustlers. But J. J.'s career took on another dimension when he went international; it was by expanding his horizons that he became infamous.

A story illustrating Johnston's notoriety was supplied by Tony Dowling a couple of days after J. J. returned from his voyage to England with Speed Christian. (It should be mentioned that it was Johnston who had sent Dowling to defeat in Auckland, New Zealand, and Rotterdam, Holland.)

"The day after the fight I get this call from Don Majesky in London." As matchmaker for the card, headed by the Herol Graham-Johnny Melfah British middleweight championship, Majesky was personally embarrassed by the Christian-Oyebola bout. It was not so much Christian's performance in the ring but Johnston's out of it that was causing headaches for Majesky. What J. J. wanted was his money, which the British Commission was attempting to withhold pending an investigation. J. J. was seen to be making a nuisance of himself. "So," Dowling continues, "Majesky says to me, 'Tony, you know this guy. You got to talk to him and get him out of here.' Well, I did my best."

Johnston simply laughs when I ask him about this. "Hey, I like London. I wanted to stay around awhile. I'll tell you something; before the bout, they asked me, 'Mr. Johnston, over the years how many fighters have you brought to England?' 'Nine counting this one,' I told them. 'And how many of those have won?' 'Sir,' I said to him, 'tomorrow night will be the first.' "

Not that J. J. goes *looking* for international trouble, you understand. He claims it is always thrust upon him, and offers the following story as evidence. "I had been looking for an overseas fight for any of my guys and finally—probably to shut me up for a while—Hank Ruehling, the European promoter, asked me if I had a decent light heavyweight. Well, I did. Ruehling says the guy has to weigh 170 pounds, give or take a pound. I call the fighter—I won't mention any names—and he says he weighs 171 exactly. Okay, I call Ruehling and he says to bring him over. To Belgium.

"When I get to the Toronto airport with the fighter, there is a scale and I have him get on it, and he only weighs 165. I call Ruehling and tell him I'm sorry but the guy is actually too light so we can't come after all. Ruehling tells me not to worry about it. 'It'll be taken care of,' is what he said." At this point in the tale, Johnston assumes his most blameless expression. "Well, we get to Brussels and the night before the weigh-in there's a knock on the door. I open it and a guy hands me lead weights and a needle and thread, and tells me to sew them into the fighter's trunks."

But the central incident in the Johnston catalogue of infamy concerns a supposed dive one of his fighters took in Amsterdam. The press, both here and in Holland, made Johnston out to be a villain, accusing him not only of supplying false information about his man's record but also of counselling the fighter to go into the tank. Johnston pleads innocence and you tend to believe him, if only because he takes a measure of honest delight in his ruses and freely confesses to them. For instance, he admits, with some irony, that the only thing he did wrong in

Amsterdam was to give Jerry Reddick, known as Mac Truck, a rock to put in his trunks to make the weight. "Jerry told me he was a full-fledged light heavy but we get there and he's only 161. The weigh-in's at eleven o'clock. I go out looking for some lead weights but all the stores are closed in Amsterdam on Monday morning. I was passing a construction site and," he shrugs, "I happened to see this rock."

Johnston's version of what happened in the Dutch capital is quite different from the media's. "It all started with a call I got from Pat O'Grady, the head of the World Athletic Association. Over here we know that doesn't mean anything but in Europe it carries a little bit of weight. O'Grady wants to stage the WAA light heavyweight championship and asks me for three names. I give him the three, one of which is Reddick. He calls me back a few days later and says to bring Reddick over to fight for the championship."

Reddick had been the middleweight winner of the first Tough Guy contest on the west coast. He turned pro and ran up a string of victories. With his bald dome, flashy style and engaging manner around the media, he was quite popular for a couple of years. Then he seemed to lose interest in the sport and fought sporadically. When Johnston telephoned him in Calgary, Reddick told him he had fought a year earlier in Halifax. J. J. relayed the information to O'Grady, who thought it sufficed and sent the tickets.

"In the meantime," says J. J., "I had gone out to Calgary to look Reddick over. Not wanting to send any stiffs to Amsterdam, you see. Jerry told me he had been training and he looked to be in shape. That is, he looked in shape when I finally got a chance to see him work out. He kept hanging me up. I waited around for five days and had to hock my diamond ring to pay the hotel bill.

"We went to Amsterdam and everything went all right until the morning of the fight when I went to the coffee shop with Reddick's girl friend. He brought this twenty-year-old blonde with him. She says, 'What's going to happen tonight?' I says, 'I don't know; he's been training, hasn't he?' And she says, 'No way. And he didn't fight last year either.' So I consult the record book and see his last fight was actually twenty-one months earlier when he got stopped by Wayne Caplette. I says to him, 'Jerry, you lied to me,' and he shrugged. 'Are you in any kind of shape, or what?' and he says, 'No, man, I ain't in shape. What should I do?' I says, 'Well, your only chance, you got to try and knock him out in the first round.'

"Anyway, the fight starts and he makes it through the first round, but he's exhausted. In the second round he goes down. Afterwards everybody said he went in the tank. They held up the purse and we all three got stranded there. But then Jerry starts playing to them. He makes money going on TV and talking about it. He tells them what they want to hear. He tells them that he didn't try. But he did, and he got hurt bad, too. He really got hit hard. He's five-nine, by the way, and the other guy was six-three. He's having himself a good time, and making some money. Him and the girl, they even went to the Canadian consulate and got a hundred dollars each. Finally our tickets were validated. It was probably embarrassing for them to have us around. We left."

Back in Vancouver, the press heaped scorn on Johnston, declaring he had made his fighter take a dive. They used him as an example of much that they found wrong with boxing. "I fought the case for two years. Finally the officials declared there was no evidence to suggest Reddick took a dive. I brought the letters that stated their decision to the newspapers here, to the same guys who had accused me without proof. But they wouldn't print anything exonerating me." Then, his eyes twinkling, J. J. says, "As for that accusation that I sent an impostor to fight in South Africa, why . . . that . . . well, that's . . . it's the truth. There *were* extenuating circumstances."

Johnston admits to having had a good time in boxing. And

it's a good thing too, because he's never made much money. "Oh, I made *some* money, of course. But after forty years, adding it up, I haven't come out ahead of the game. I lost on the promotions, especially; but I never did any of it for the *money*. I had a ball going to all those places, seeing so many fights, meeting all those people.

"I tell you, I've come across a lot of colourful people in boxing, guys like Chris and Angelo Dundee, Irving Ungerman, Dewey Fregosa, Hank Ruehling, Hank Kaplan. Real characters. But the best of them all was the Mayor of Tap City. They don't make them like that anymore."

Nick Zubray, the Mayor of Tap City. Not only do they not make them like that any more, they didn't make all that many of them to begin with.

I remember stepping off the ferry in the spring of 1982, back on the mainland after the Racette-Berbick fight, picking up the paper and reading about Nick taking the long count. A phone call from Edmonton informed me that several people had gotten together after the services to sprinkle champagne over his memory. Among them were fellow rounders, hustlers and wise guys, as well as media types who could always salvage an uninspired Edmonton winter day with a story about the mayor. Hey, how about the time Nick wanted to build a dome-covered playground so that Edmonton nudists could sunbathe without the distraction of mosquitoes?

Many of those present at the reception hoped to catch a little of his reflection. Zubray was a guy who hosted press conferences in a white suit with a pink carnation, poured pink champagne, told tales for a couple of hours, then almost as an afterthought announced the reason for the gathering: a boxing card in the Kootenays or a wrestling extravaganza in Prince Albert. These contests were of lesser consequence, of no consequence, really, at least in the scheme of things, except that they provided the means by which Nick added to his store of stories. If some of the tales were apocryphal, it matters not at all, because those were indistinguishable from the real ones.

I only met the guy once, unfortunately, and that was at his then current residence, a room at the Macdonald Hotel. It may have been Edmonton outside but he was dressed for Rio de Janeiro, and he looked like he had just stepped off the cover of *Gentleman's Quarterly*—a 1938 issue. He was sharp, in other words, in a tropical sense, in white suit and shoes, wide Countess Mara tie, carnation, and pink handkerchief in his breast pocket. He had an enormous head, a battered face, a neck like a tree stump and black, patent-leather hair. When his blunt hands moved there was a flashing of gold, silver and coloured stones. Until he started to talk, Nick might have been taken for a guy who had made a million dollars with those hands and then kept his fingers manicured forever after. But once he started talking you realized work was something he refused to have any part of, just as a million dollars would have no part of him. The suits—there was a closet full of them—were for the purpose of keeping up a front so he could keep making his game. "Always look sharp," he advised. "If you can't go first class, look like you are."

I had been dispatched to see Nick by a political type from another city who was the anonymous backer of a certain prize fighter. The idea was to come up with a plan to promote this guy as well as to get him on a card that Nick was staging in Edmonton. Nick thought of twenty ways to tout the fighter in the first ten minutes, each more extravagant than the last, and all redolent of a carnival side show in Fort St. John in a simpler era. But the pugilist was soon forgotten as Nick poured the Chateau-Gai and started spinning yarns. While he talked, Mario Lanza sang in the background on a record player atop a suitcase. There were other grips lined up near the door, as if Nick were liable to split at any moment. When it was necessary to flip a record over, Nick burst into song himself so the music wouldn't stop. And it was a fine voice he had, too.

He spoke his own language, and you can't mention Nick without references to tap city, ankle express and polyester millionaires, the latter being the well-heeled squares he endeavoured to separate from their long green. And then there was his marvellously inventive manner of cursing. He somehow managed to be vile and genial at the same time. He told me about the time he was in Toronto dealing with Irving Ungerman on the promotion of the Ali-Chuvalo fight. A guy accosted him on the street, and Nick, a former wrestler, pushed the guy away. Unfortunately, the man's trajectory took him through a plate-glass window. Nick made a quick departure via ankle express, but the cops nabbed him near the entrance to his hotel. As they were taking him away, he was hollering, "Ungerman . . . Chuvalo . . . Ali!" The police thought he was a maniac and had decided to deliver him to the appropriate facility at 999 Queen Street West. "It didn't get cleared up until I got Chuvalo on the phone."

It has been said that Nick was a bad-luck guy. But it was not garden-variety bad luck he had. No, it was as if a special, diabolical brand had been devised just for him. *Bad* luck is having a fight card snowed out, the snow so deep and heavy folks can't get to the venue; *Nick's* luck was having a Lethbridge fight card snowed out in July. He once put together a promoter's nightmare, six first-round knockouts. Nick had the western Canada closed-circuit rights to the Patterson-Chuvalo fight, and the picture failed. Another time, he got Vancouver stock promoter Murray Pezim to back him for the local closed-circuit telecast of the Ali-Mac Foster fight only to discover the bout was on cable TV from Seattle.

It may surprise some to hear that Nick was unfailingly honest. True, he might at times of necessity take French leave from pecuniary embarrassment, but he always rectified the situation. For instance, after an entire year of living in the Mayfair Hotel in Vancouver, he split owing the establishment $10,000. A year passed, during which time the hotel had given up any notion of gaining restitution. Then one day in walks Nick Zubray, peels off one hundred one-hundreds, and gives them to an astonished cashier.

"Here's the way Nick's career went," says Jimmy Johnston. "He was handling promotions over here for Ali's fiasco with the Japanese wrestler Ioki. He hired me to put up posters for him and offered me $18 an hour. This was in the early seventies. I said, 'Nick, that's a lot of money.' He said, 'Jimmy, you're worth it and a lot more.' "

But the next time they met up, Nick was tap city. "He was short and I lent him fifty bucks. A week or so later, he's back in town and calls me up, takes me to dinner. We have a fine meal at a nice Italian restaurant and he picks up the cheque and gives me the fifty I had lent him. Then he hands me a box with a brand-new pair of shoes inside. 'What's this?' I say. Nick says, 'Oh, I remembered we take the same size.' "

You might have seen Nick loitering on the corner of Tap City one afternoon, but by that evening he could be waving to you from a Cadillac on his way to the bright lights. Some of his cronies say that Nick was not in his usual high spirits that last year. But he was a refugee from another time, forever chasing the fast buck, around and around the corner in a franchise world. He knew it, but had a hard time admitting that the world was passing his kind by. However, the sympathy the commentators felt for him was misplaced. Even in his current condition, Nick Zubray seems more alive than half the citizens on the bricks.

"Ah, what I've liked more than anything," Tony Dowling is saying, "has been listening to the old guys. The characters telling stories and bullshitting. Wherever I was, I'd get them to talk, and how they could talk. I didn't realize it, but as I was fighting here and managing there, travelling to this place and that, I was getting my own stories to tell. I guess I became a character myself. But I'm through with it now. There's nothing happening. To hell with it."

"But what if you found a kid, a good prospect, one who really wanted to do it, and wanted you to manage him. Wouldn't you get involved?"

"Damned right, I would. I love it. Boxing gets in your blood and doesn't get out."